Effectively Designed Instruction

Effectively Designed Instruction

Amplifying Student Agency and Inclusivity

Samuel Mormando

ConnectEDD Publishing
Hanover, Pennsylvania

This publication is available at discount pricing when purchased in quantity for educational purposes, promotions, or fundraisers. For inquiries and details, contact the publisher at: info@connecteddpublishing.com

Published by ConnectEDD Publishing LLC
Hanover, PA
www.connecteddpublishing.com

Cover Design: Kheila Casas

Effectively Designed Instruction by Samuel Mormando. —1st ed.
Paperback ISBN 979-8-9890027-0-2

ConnectEDD
PUBLISHING

Praise for *Effectively Designed Instruction*

Discover the transformative power of student-centered instructional design. This book is an essential read for educators and instructional designers looking to create engaging, meaningful, and effective learning experiences. Get ready to empower your students and revolutionize your teaching approach!

—Julie Devine | Supervisor of Digital and Online Learning

Effectively Designed Instruction is an excellent addition to any teacher's professional library. This book is a concise and invaluable guide for educators seeking to enhance their teaching methods. Dr. Mormando's insights and practical tips are essential for anyone passionate about effective instruction that meets their students' needs.

—Christine Gumpert | K-12 Instructional Coach

Effectively Designed Instruction is a must read. It meets teachers where they are and expands their knowledge on inclusivity, content presentation, experiences, and interactions. This book provides practical strategies to create inclusive classrooms, deliver engaging content, craft meaningful learning experiences, and foster dynamic and authentic interactions.

—Dr. Adam Penning | Elementary School Principal

If you want to know how to reach each and every student while keeping your life and work balanced, this is the book for you. Sam's experience and expertise with crafting student-centered instruction shines through in every chapter. No matter who, where, or what you teach, this book has something that will help you reach students more effectively. Through the simple techniques he outlines, you can take your teaching to a whole new level without exhausting yourself in the process.

—Dr. Leslee Hutchinson | Assistant Superintendent of Schools

I wholeheartedly endorse Dr. Sam Mormando's book, *Effectively Designed Instruction*. His book is a practical, no-nonsense guide that equips educators with the tools they need to create a more effective and inclusive learning environment for their students. What sets this book apart is the way Dr. Mormando seamlessly weaves together theory and real-life examples from his own journey in education. Having had the privilege of working closely with him for the past four years, I've witnessed the transformative impact of his methods firsthand. *Effectively Designed Instruction* provides teachers with practical strategies and insights that can be implemented immediately to enhance their instructional delivery. Whether you're a seasoned educator or just starting your teaching journey, this book is a quick and helpful guide that empowers you to make meaningful improvements in your practice.

—Dr. Haley Butler | High School Assistant Principal

This transformative guide to post-pandemic education has reshaped my approach to how we professionally develop our teachers. The book's passionate call to let go of old mindsets resonated deeply, enabling my team to begin to adapt our curricula to our new normal.

—Dr. Emily Thompson | Superintendent of Schools

This book was a revelation for our special education department. The comprehensive dive into the EDI framework illuminated the path to true inclusivity. Now, every child in our care receives tailor-made instruction, and the results are astounding. I appreciated the connection between EDI and UDL which makes it all the more actionable for our teachers.

—Elizabeth Hughes | Special Education Coordinator

Math instruction has taken on a new life in my classroom. Through the vivid integration strategies—especially the use of videos—my students now have an easier time grasping complex concepts with ease. An eye catching and transformative read!

—Sophie DiMartinez | 8th Grade Mathematics Teacher

Navigating the post-pandemic educational terrain feels daunting, but this book was a huge help in getting me to think differently. Its emphasis on video integration was a revelation, even for my brick-and-mortar teachers. I've since shared these strategies with dozens of colleagues to try for themselves.

—Jason Mitchell | Technology Integration Specialist

I've immersed myself in this treasure! I was captivated by its focus on fostering deep student connections. Applying the feedback strategies with my university students, I've witnessed a renewed zest in their learning. They're more engaged, expressive, and responsive. This book is a must have for anyone in education.

—Dr. Isabelle Kim | Professor of Educational Leadership

I was struck by the idea that inclusivity is the "heartbeat of your classroom." We teach students with many barriers to their learning: social-emotional, executive functioning, and diversity of needs. This book recognizes these barriers and offers real world solutions that are not only applicable in school, but to their future learning and place in society.

—Lynn Cashell | 5th Grade Teacher

A perfect blend of theory and practice, this book offers a crystal-clear blueprint for post-pandemic instruction. Adopting its methodologies, I've crafted online courses that resonate deeply with both adolescent and adult learners.

—Dr. Natalie Foster | Researcher in Adaptive Learning Strategies

This book masterfully dissects the challenges of online and blended learning and offers innovative solutions to solve them. My team's lessons have already transformed, resulting in heightened student engagement and better learning experiences.

—Benjamin Gray | Online Learning Coordinator

EDI streamlines all the current research and frameworks in use today and packages them into four easy to understand elements. As a busy middle school teacher, I'm able to incorporate these strategies into my lesson planning so that my students get the best learning experience possible.

—Angela Peterson | 7th Grade Literacy Teacher

We all want to engage our students and drive efficacy and achievement. But how, in a world where everything is changing and lots of shiny tools can distract us? Mormando has the answer in this thought-provoking book: focus on what we can control and impact—effectively designed instruction. This book is for all the educators who want to better their craft in order to create epic learning experiences for our kids.

—AJ Juliani | Best-selling Author and Founder *Adaptable Learning*

Effectively Designed Instruction unlocks the secret to fostering student agency and inclusivity. This book brilliantly shows us how to inspire and engage our learners, empowering students to take control of their learning journeys. With practical strategies and heartfelt insights, it positions teaching and learning as collaborative adventures. For educators seeking to create meaningful, student-centered classrooms, this book belongs on your "to be read" list!

—Meghan Lowe | K-12 Instructional Coach

It's not every day that you come across a book that truly has the power to transform the way we approach education. *Effectively Designed Instruction* is one such remarkable masterpiece that promises to redefine the art of teaching and learning.

—Dr. Joseph Kingsborough | High School Administrator

Effectively Designed Instruction offers practical, easy to implement strategies for teachers to create engaging lessons while empowering learners and promoting inclusivity. With clear themes and an accessible tone, it simplifies lesson planning while maximizing impact. *Effectively Designed Instruction* is a game-changer for educators seeking to transform their classrooms.

—Katie Bienkowski | Ed.D.

Mormando expertly shares a masterclass that reimagines how we create engaging and inclusive experiences for every learner. Whether you're in education or not, you'll be inspired by entrepreneurial stories with practical strategies to take action in creating learning experiences that deliver effective and equitable results.

—Dr. Aparna Ramanathan | EdTech Startup Founder and CEO, Silicon Valley

At the core of EDI is the belief that quality instruction is the balance between intentional design and effective delivery. This book will transform teaching and learning in the post-pandemic era. With an emphasis on the four themes: Designing Experiences, Building Interactions,

Presenting Content and Accessibility and Inclusion, EDI equips teachers with highly effective instructional strategies they need to thrive in the classroom and meet students' diverse learning needs. An essential guide for all educators!

—Nikolette Trofa | K-12 Instructional Coach

In an era where educators grapple with a multitude of initiatives, this groundbreaking book is indispensable. It provides practical strategies for teachers and school leaders to seamlessly integrate various components of seemingly disparate initiatives into their instructional design and delivery and ultimately engage and empower all students to take charge of their learning.

—Dr. Lauren Hopkins | Supervisor of Secondary Humanities

Dr. Sam Mormando's *Effectively Designed Instruction* is a beacon of wisdom for educators. It's a refreshing departure from fleeting trends, focusing on timeless strategies that define excellent teaching. Whether you're a novice or a seasoned teacher, this book offers practical insights that resonate with the real challenges teachers face today. His guidance on fostering student agency, reflective learning, and constructive feedback is invaluable. From structuring materials in a learning management system to nurturing parental involvement, this book is a comprehensive guide to creating an inclusive learning environment. A must-read for educators committed to maximizing student potential.

—Kimberly J. Hassel-Kloss, M.Ed. | Assistant Director of
    Special Education

Effectively Designed Instruction is a critical component of meeting the diverse needs of learners in our evolving world. This book is thoughtfully designed for educators and provides a rich balance of examples that will ignite passion in educators and students alike.

> —Katie Martin | Cofounder & Chief Impact Officer, Learner-Center Collaborative, author of Learner-Centered Innovation and Evolving Education

Effectively Designed Instruction creates a paradigm shift of not designing for the middle and then differentiating up and down, but rather rethinking how we design instruction for all students right from the beginning. Dr. Mormando provides easy to remember themes that pull together important frameworks that are made practical and alive with vivid examples from real teachers, classrooms, and students.

> —Dr. Zora M. Wolfe | Associate Professor, K-12 Educational Leadership, Widener University

My first-hand experience learning from Sam Mormando about his principles of *Effectively Designed Instruction* (EDI) parallels the lessons he conveys in this book. EDI is about a mindset shift with a bevy of practical instructional strategies to promote personalization through agency for the 21st-century learner. Mormando's student-focused advice melds the well-known instructional underpinnings of blended learning, differentiated instruction, and Universally Designed Learning (UDL) with the intentional use of educational technology. Sam and his team's work with my school district has spawned our Empowered Teacher's Academy - rooted in EDI. This book provides sensible solutions to relatable instructional design issues to support classroom teachers and school leaders in tackling the shared responsibility for educating today's students.

> —Emily Virga | Chief Academic Officer, Kingsway Regional SD

Table of Contents

Preface

"Teaching is the one profession that creates all other professions, for it equips individuals with the knowledge, skills, and inspiration they need to pursue their dreams and shape the world around them. It is a noble and transformative endeavor that holds the power to unlock infinite possibilities and leave an indelible impact on generations to come."

–Daniel J. Boorstin

Navigating the Complex Terrain of Personalized Learning

If you are like me, sometimes the goal to personalize the learning experience for students, especially when it comes to students with different learning needs, can seem almost impossible. It's not that anyone would disagree with the need to educate students in the least restrictive environment or provide students with the accommodations or modifications they need to comprehend the course material. It's that educating all students, based on each student's particular learning preference and unique needs, is extremely complex.

So, if some of your students lack enthusiasm for class, slouch in their seat, or become easily distracted by their phone or laptop, I'm right with you. Teaching has never been more difficult than it is today. Teachers are tasked with disproportionate workloads and often competing responsibilities, making it difficult to provide adequate support for every student on their roster. Special education teachers are especially vulnerable to this role overload due to the wide range of job responsibilities and administrative paperwork being pushed down from the federal and state levels. These are just some of the reasons for the increase in teacher attrition rates. For some, the added stress of trying to personalize learning for such a diverse group of students has understandably led to increased burnout, a decrease in overall productivity, and even lower expectations for the overall classroom.

The result is often to "teach to the middle" and create lessons for the "average" student, then try to differentiate up or down based on results from a formative or summative assessment. This technique has been widely accepted because there is only so much one teacher can do on any given day, right? The question I often hear as a school administrator is how can one teacher possibly personalize the learning experience for twenty-five different students? The answer is, by approaching these issues in the same ways that we always have, it's impossible.

The problem, as I see it, is when we teach to the middle or when we try to design for the average student, we actually design for no one. Todd Rose, the director of the Mind, Brain, and Education program at the Harvard Graduate School of Education, explains in his book, *The End of Average* (2016), that measuring individuals against the theoretical average actually hurts everyone. In his book, Dr. Rose uses the example of the United States Air Force following World War II to drive home this point.

He explains that during the 1950s, the United States Air Force realized that the design of the cockpit was causing pilots to have difficulty controlling their planes. Initially, the problem was attributed to pilot error and poor training. It was eventually determined that the one-size-fits-all cockpit design was not suitable for the pilots of the 1950s, who had different dimensions than pilots of the 1920s. The Air Force measured the dimensions of over 4,000 pilots and found that none fit the average range on any of the dimensions used to design the cockpits.

Instead, every pilot had a unique profile, with different combinations of their physical dimensions. As a result, the Air Force banned the use of the average and mandated that manufacturers design cockpits that were adjustable for the extremes in size and shape rather than just what was believed to be the dimensions of the average pilot. This required manufacturers to create options such as adjustable seats, controls, and pedals. Predictably, following the redesign, the pilots' performance exceeded every measure.

It seems we're making the same mistake in education that the Air Force made in the 1950s. Instead of looking at design and fit the way the Air Force did, many so-called educational experts blame teachers, blame students, and blame parents for the problems in our schools. As if the problem in education today is any of those things. What if, like the cockpit problem in the 1950s, a key issue in education today is bad design?

Perhaps you remember the push towards flexible classroom seating not too long ago. In many schools, particularly in elementary classrooms, the standard-size desk, standard-size chair, and standard-size table were replaced with adjustable-height desks, chairs with swinging footrests, collaboration tables, and multi-colored soft cushion seats. Just as we addressed the need to create flexible classroom spaces, it's time to rethink the way we design and deliver our instruction so it, too, can be as flexible as our classroom furniture. By doing so, we'll be able to meet the needs of individual students and account for all the unique characteristics students bring to our classroom.

To make it happen, we'll need to *Effectively Design Instruction*. Meaning, we'll need to proactively account for the extremes in learner variability and create learning experiences that take into account the diverse learning styles and unique needs of all our students—from gifted to on grade-level to those who need special education services and support.

When we *Effectively Design Instruction*, we are intentional about meeting the needs of every student under our care. This means considering the diverse learning styles of students, such as visual learners, auditory learners, and kinesthetic learners, and finding ways to incorporate multiple learning modalities into our lessons. It also means being aware of the unique challenges and needs of our students, such as students with learning disabilities, students with language barriers, and students who may be struggling with mental health issues.

Effectively Designed Instruction requires us to be creative and flexible in our approach to teaching. It means being willing to try new things and adapt our lessons, as needed, in order to meet the needs of the students who sit in our classrooms, whether that be the physical classroom or the virtual one. It also means being open to feedback and constantly looking for ways to improve our instruction. By *Effectively Designing Instruction*, we can finally create learning experiences that are more engaging, inclusive, and personalized. This approach helps us move away from teaching to the middle and allows us to truly maximize student agency and inclusivity, ensuring that all students have the opportunity to thrive in school.

From Pressure to Purpose

As educators, we hold ourselves to extremely high standards, striving to provide the best possible learning experiences for our students. At the same time, we face mounting expectations from various stakeholders, including our school communities, policymakers, and even society itself. It's a delicate balance, and we often find ourselves caught in the middle as we navigate the pressures of our profession.

From the relentless pressures of No Child Left Behind to the latest iteration of the Danielson Framework, the ever-evolving landscape of education can leave many educators feeling like they're carrying the weight of the world on their shoulders. And that's just the tip of the iceberg. With the world rapidly changing around us, we're tasked with adapting our teaching methods to keep up with new technology, societal shifts, and unprecedented challenges like the COVID-19 pandemic.

But what if there were a way to not only meet these high expectations but to excel in the midst of them? In this book, we'll explore practical strategies and innovative approaches that will empower you to rise above the challenges and create a learning environment where both you and your students can thrive.

The stakes in getting this right have never been higher—not just for individual teachers but for our entire educational community. Today's teachers are at the heart of shaping our future, guiding the minds that will lead, innovate, and inspire. Yet, they often grapple with a system that can be constraining and unyielding. The weight of expectations and the ever-shifting educational landscape call for a responsive, adaptable approach. It's more than a professional necessity; it's a moral imperative to equip teachers with the strategies, tools, and confidence they need to excel.

In our pursuit of excellence, we must recognize and respond to the unique challenges educators face, ensuring they have the resources and support necessary to foster a nurturing, engaging, and effective learning environment. As a teacher, coach, and school administrator, I have a front-row seat to the daily challenges teachers face. With this book, I aim to equip educators across the country with practical, research-based strategies and approaches centered around maximizing student agency and inclusivity. Whether you're a seasoned educator or just beginning your journey in the profession, and irrespective of the subject area you teach or support, the resources in this book will empower you to create effective and engaging learning experiences adaptable to any learning format.

It Takes a Village

Education is a team effort. It takes a village of support from school boards, administrators, faculty, support staff, students, and the wider school community to make a difference in the lives of young learners. I've been fortunate to work in the supportive environment of the Garnet Valley School District (Glen Mills, Pennsylvania) for the last decade, where I've gained valuable insights and experiences that I'm excited to share with you in this book.

Throughout my career, I have been fortunate to collaborate with exceptional organizations such as International Society for Technology in Education (ISTE), Global Online Academy (GOA), and the Instructional Coaching Group (ICG). Seeing their impact on my colleagues inspired me to co-found the award-winning educational nonprofit, *Edvative Learning*, in 2018. It's through *Edvative Learning* that I get to refine my work even further and share my passion for intentional instructional design with educators across the world.

These experiences have allowed me to work alongside hundreds of extraordinary educators, all driven by their passion to personalize education and harness the power of intentional instructional design. In the chapters that follow, I will share with you the valuable insights and innovative work of many of these dedicated professionals and try my best to shine a light on their amazing work. I will also interlace real-life experiences and stories from other thought leaders to reinforce the notion that with purposeful and intentional planning, we can truly *Effectively Design Instruction* for every student on our roster.

But where does your journey begin? Recognizing your position on the Continuum of Classroom Design discussed in the next section is the first step. Whether you find yourself in the traditional classroom setting, experimenting with the aesthetically driven "Pretty for Pinterest" phase, or striving towards the pinnacle of effective instructional design, this book is your guide. Through my experiences at Garnet

Valley and *Edvative Learning,* I've observed thousands of educators, each at different stages, but all united by a common goal: to evolve, adapt, and create learning environments that truly meet the needs of every student. Together, we'll explore the strategies, methods, and real-life examples that will empower you to transform your instruction and maximize every student's potential.

The Continuum of Classroom Design

Traditional Classroom Instruction	"Pretty for Pinterest"	Effectively Designed Instruction
• Teacher-centered learning • Standardized assessment • Fixed curriculum • Lecture as the primary mode of instruction • Minimal technology use • Little to no individualized learning paths • Passive student participation	• Decorative, aesthetically pleasing elements • Surface-level technology integration • Trendy teaching ideas that may or may not enhance learning • Greater emphasis on creativity, but not always connected to pedagogy • Some elements of active learning, but lacks a comprehensive, student-centered approach • May incorporate diverse materials but lacks deliberate inclusivity strategies	• Learner-centered pedagogy • Use of various assessment methods for a comprehensive understanding of learning • Flexibility in the curriculum to adapt to individual needs • Active learning strategies • Integration of appropriate technology to enhance learning • Individualized learning paths to maximize student agency • Active student participation and collaboration • Inclusive materials and strategies, catering to diverse student backgrounds and needs

The traditional classroom represents the starting point on this continuum. Here, instruction is primarily teacher-centered, with lecture as the dominant mode of content delivery. Assessment practices are standardized, and curricula are fixed, offering little flexibility to accommodate individual learning needs. While this method can be practical and straightforward, it often overlooks students' unique learning styles, backgrounds, and needs, limiting their active engagement and personal agency in their learning journey.

Moving along the continuum, we encounter what Thomas Murray, author of *Personal & Authentic* calls the "Pretty for Pinterest" phase. This stage is characterized by an increased emphasis on aesthetics and creative elements. It attempts to break free from traditional molds, incorporating trendy teaching ideas and surface-level technology integration. However, despite its appeal and well-intentioned efforts, this phase often lacks a meaningful connection between creativity and pedagogy. Inclusivity and student agency may still fall short due to an absence of comprehensive, evidence-based strategies.

At the far end of the continuum lies Effectively Designed Instruction (EDI). This is our desired destination. Here, the classroom transforms into an environment where instruction is learner-centered, inclusive, and adaptive. Teachers employ diverse assessment methods to provide a holistic understanding of student progress and individualized learning paths. Active learning strategies and appropriate technology use are integrated *purposefully*. The curriculum is flexible and evolves to cater to each student's unique needs, fostering active participation and maximizing student agency.

By reading this book, teachers will be guided along this continuum, from their current position to the desired destination. Each chapter provides practical strategies, research-backed methods, and real-life examples to help educators transform their instruction. The goal is not just to make classrooms prettier or trendier, but to make them more responsive and inclusive, thereby maximizing every student's potential. By the end of this journey, teachers will be empowered to design and implement lessons that foster agency, engagement, and inclusivity, ultimately creating a learning environment that meets the needs of every student.

Introduction

*"The most powerful principle in teaching is to treat each
student as a unique individual. No two students are exactly
alike, and what works for one student may not work for another.
It is important to remember that each student comes to the classroom
with different backgrounds, experiences, and needs."*

–Robert John Meehan

Let's Begin by Recognizing Learner Variability

As an educator, it is essential to recognize that all students have varying ways of perceiving, understanding, and processing information. No two students are the same, and each brings their own set of experiences, skills, and learning styles to the classroom. Failing to recognize this fact makes it impossible to personalize learning.

One particularly memorable experience that illustrates the importance of *Effectively Designed Instruction* took place when I was teaching a unit on metropolitan growth in the Philadelphia region to a group of 10th grade students at Penn Wood High School in Lansdowne, Pennsylvania. Despite putting in many hours of preparation and crafting engaging activities and materials that I thought would appeal to all my students, I quickly realized that not everyone was on the same page.

One student, Tiara, was struggling to grasp the concepts, appeared disengaged in the lessons, and was acting out in class. I hadn't realized at the time, but Tiara's behavior was getting worse as the year progressed. Upon closer observation, I noticed that she was having difficulty focusing and seemed to be zoning out no matter the activity. I recognized that the situation wasn't getting better on its own and that I needed to make a change, or I was going to lose Tiara for the remainder of the school year.

After speaking with Tiara and her parents, I discovered that she had been diagnosed with ADHD and struggled with attention and focus in school since she was young. It became clear that my lessons were not designed with her needs in mind, and I needed to find a way to adapt my teaching style to better support her.

In an effort to help Tiara, I broke down the material into smaller chunks and incorporated more hands-on activities and visual aids to help her better understand the concepts. I began by dividing the lesson into smaller sub-topics such as historical context, population growth, economic factors, and urban planning. I then began incorporating videos, interactive maps, and images to cater to her learning needs.

I also provided Tiara with additional support and accommodations, such as allowing her to take breaks as needed and providing her with a fidget toy to help her focus. These changes made a significant difference for Tiara; by the end of the unit, she was much more engaged in my lessons, had a better understanding of the material, and no longer exhibited disruptive behavior in class. What I didn't realize at the time was that my efforts to help Tiara had a positive impact on other students as well. Even those without specific learning disabilities benefitted from the diverse teaching methods, such as videos and interactive maps, that were implemented to cater to Tiara's needs.

This experience was not just a one-off event for Tiara. Two years after graduation and upon acceptance into Temple University, she placed a note in my school mailbox. The note read:

Dear Mr. M.,

I just wanted to thank you for being such an amazing teacher and role model. When I first came to Penn Wood, I was really struggling to understand myself. I thought I was dumb, my teachers thought I was bad, and my parents didn't know what to think of me. I was suspended at least twice in 10th grade (one wasn't my fault!) and I was really thinking about dropping out. But you took the time to get to know me and understand me. Not just me, everyone in the class. But for me, you saw I had a different way to learn, and you made changes to the way you taught the class to better help me. No one had ever done that before. I don't know how else to say it, but thank you for recognizing my needs as a student. It was the first time any teacher really cared enough to allow me to be me, and not punish me for being different. I'm headed to Temple next year, but I will come to visit your classroom when home. BTW, I still use the fidget toy you gave me.

Your favorite student (HAHA)
Tiara

Tiara's note reinforced for me the significance of considering the unique needs of all students and being willing to adapt and make changes to meet those needs. While Tiara's story is just one example of how *Effectively Designed Instruction* can make a significant impact on a student's life, it underscores the importance of considering individual student needs, even if it means making changes to the curriculum or providing additional support and accommodations to help them succeed.

Lessons Learned from the Virtual Classroom

The unprecedented COVID-19 pandemic upended educational systems around the world. The United Nations Educational, Scientific, and Cultural Organization (UNESCO) reported that 90% of the world's educational systems were forced to transition to virtual learning due to the pandemic. The public education system in the United States, like many other countries, was not fully prepared for this transition. Consequently, over forty-six million public school students in the U.S. were forced to learn in a virtual format with no preparation for this learning modality.

As schools rushed to adopt virtual learning for their students, disparities between school districts and among subgroups of students within those districts started to surface. In a RAND Corporation report published in the spring of 2020, researchers found widespread differences in how districts supported their staff and students during the pandemic. This report found that most teachers surveyed did not receive adequate guidance and support to address students' needs in a virtual learning environment. This number was even higher for teachers working with students identified with a disability.

In my district, it felt like 2015 all over again. Despite having several years under our belts running our own virtual program and having close to a thousand students take classes in this format, when COVID hit, it was like we were starting over from scratch. One thing was clear: there is a BIG difference between educating students who *opt* into virtual learning and teaching students who were *forced* into it. This is true for parents as well. Every school has countless examples of students shutting down, turning off their cameras, or not showing up for virtual learning during the pandemic.

While working with teachers in the Interboro School District (Prospect Park, Pennsylvania) during the pandemic, I witnessed many challenges some students faced when transitioning to virtual learning.

One student, in particular, struggled with this transition. Prior to the pandemic, Rachel was a highly engaged and motivated student. She was always prepared for class and participated actively in discussions. However, when Interboro High School made the transition to virtual learning, Rachel seemed to struggle more than others. She frequently missed live sessions, struggled to stay focused during class, and fell behind on her assignments. Essentially, Rachel went from being a member of the National Honor Society to failing all her courses in a matter of weeks.

As teachers tried to support Rachel, they realized that she was struggling with several challenges that were making it difficult for her to succeed in a virtual learning environment. For one, she lived in a household with several younger siblings who were also learning virtually, and it was difficult for her to find a quiet space to focus on her work. In addition, Rachel was struggling with some personal issues that were affecting her ability to concentrate and stay motivated. As a way to support Rachel, her teachers met with her parents and together, they created a schedule that allowed her to have dedicated time to focus on her schoolwork. They also provided her with additional resources and accommodations, such as extra time to complete assignments and the option to work on assignments at her own pace. These changes made a big difference for Rachel, as she was able to catch up and get back on track before the end of the school year.

As teachers, it is our responsibility to recognize and address the unique challenges that our students may be facing, whether it be distractions at home or personal struggles that are affecting their ability to learn. This requires us to be intentional with our design and take into account the variability of learners and provide accommodations and resources that support student success.

Rachel's story is a testament to the importance of intentional instructional design and the need for educators to be flexible and adaptable in their approach to teaching. As we navigate the rapidly changing educational landscape, it is imperative that we continue to prioritize student agency and inclusivity when creating learning experiences for our students. The lessons learned during the pandemic should serve as a reminder of the importance of meeting the unique needs of all learners, and designing effective instruction to ensure that no student is left behind.

Intentional Design + Effective Delivery = Quality Instruction

The difficulties educators experienced during and after the pandemic is a failure of our educational system— not schools, not principals, and certainly not teachers. Inequitable access to technology, inconsistent funding, and the lack of federal and state support during the pandemic left many schools treading water.

Even before the pandemic, teachers were overwhelmed with balancing federal and state mandates, district initiatives, and school-specific goals that landed squarely on their shoulders. Recognizing this, I was part of a team at Garnet Valley that created the EDI framework—with the goal to help tie together all those mandates and initiatives and to help support teachers with what we believed was good teaching. This team consisted of Julie Devine, Supervisor of Digital and Online Learning, and our four Instructional Design Coaches: Mike Simone, Christine Gumpert, Meg Hayes, and Nikki Trofa. Over time, this team grew to include four additional coaches, Dr. Kate Bienkowski, Amy Rossi, Kristen Reid, and Meg Lowe, and Curriculum Supervisors, Kyle Brun and Kris LaFave. I would also be remiss if I didn't acknowledge our Superintendent, Dr. Marc Bertrando, and Assistant Superintendents, Dr. Leslee Hutchinson and Dr. Vincent Citarelli, for their role in shaping the structures of EDI.

The four themes of EDI provide a structure to help teachers personalize the learning experience for students. While the EDI framework is not intended to be all-encompassing, it is intended to provide a structure for what good teaching and intentional instructional design should look like in classrooms today.

Some may ask, with the work coming out of the pandemic, why the need to focus on instructional design now? To be honest, our administrative team wrestled with this very question. However, our work throughout the pandemic taught us this: when reduced to its simplest form, great instruction is the result of intentional design and effective delivery. Design and delivery go hand in hand; you cannot have one without the other. A well-designed lesson will go nowhere without great delivery, and a well-delivered lesson will inevitably be met with questions and confusion if not designed well.

> When reduced to its simplest form, great instruction is the result of intentional design and effective delivery.

Many schools spent the pandemic emphasizing the importance of using common nomenclature and folder structures in their school's LMS to help students access their work. These items were critical to ensuring students could easily navigate the digital classroom. Coming out of the pandemic, however, it is not enough to just focus on LMS organization. If schools are to meet the needs of every student and allow learning to take place in any format, we must focus on being intentional about how we design learning.

Intentional design is learner-centered and a way of thinking, developing, and implementing quality instruction to improve the learning experience for the end-user. It defines what and how teachers deliver their instruction, how they facilitate interactions with and between students, and how they differentiate and personalize the learning experience for the students in their classrooms. More than anything else, intentional design allows teachers to design lessons to proactively address the predictable barriers that are present in all classrooms. Subsequent sections of this book will dive deeper into this topic, but some of the predictable barriers I witness in classrooms everyday include:

> Some students may not be interested in the content or may not know why the content is important.

> Some students may have negative attitudes towards the subject, teacher, or school, which can impact their motivation and engagement.

> Some students may struggle to understand complex language or idioms, and may require translation or additional support.

> Some students may not be able to comprehend instruction if only presented in one format.

> Some students struggle to express what they really know if only given a single way to do it.

Intentional design addresses many of these issues before students even enter the classroom, ultimately making it easier for the teacher to ensure every student gets the learning experience they need. So, when I think about intentional design, I truly believe it's the most important thing teachers do to ensure the needs of every learner are being met.

Katie Novak, a leader on inclusivity and co-author of *Equity by Design*, points out that effective design allows for the "first, best instruction," before differentiation occurs and before systems of support are needed. She also does an excellent job of explaining how the focus of the design is an essential component in schools today. Katie likes to give the example of hosting a dinner party.

We have all been there. We painstakingly clean the house, buy groceries, and prep the kitchen. We then cook whatever it is we are serving at the party. But we do not just cook one meal and serve it to all our guests. That would not make much sense since it is likely that many of our guests have different tastes in foods; some may have food allergies, and some may be vegan or vegetarian. We know that going in, we cannot cook just one meal that will satisfy everyone.

So, what do we do? We may talk to the people on our guest list to see what foods they like. We may prepare different foods, anticipating that some people like certain things while others may want something different. Or we may create a buffet of sorts and provide our guests with many choices so they can create a meal that best fits their needs and preferences.

Using that analogy, we, as educators, plan a dinner party in our classroom every day. That same attention to detail and that same attention to variability at our dinner party needs to happen in our classrooms if we are truly going to meet the needs of every student. It is certainly not easy, and it will take much time and planning to be an expert designer.

I believe this book will serve as a valuable resource for teachers as they work to meet the diverse needs of their students and adapt to the changing landscape of education. The strategies discussed in this book span all course formats and apply to any learning modality.

Unlocking the Power of Effectively Designed Instruction (EDI)

The Effectively Designed Instruction (EDI) framework was originally developed to support teachers in Garnet Valley new to online and blended learning. I say originally developed because EDI has since become the foundation for how all teachers are trained in Garnet Valley and in other schools that I get the opportunity to work with through *Edvative Learning.*

In this book, we will explore the power of EDI to personalize student learning and cater to diverse student needs across all course modalities: traditional face-to-face, online, and everywhere in between. The four main themes of EDI–Building Interactions, Designing Experiences, Presenting Content, and Accessibility and Inclusion–are arranged in a non-hierarchical manner, allowing you to read or apply them in any order. For clarity and understanding, I've organized the themes in the sequence mentioned above, showcasing the interconnections between each theme.

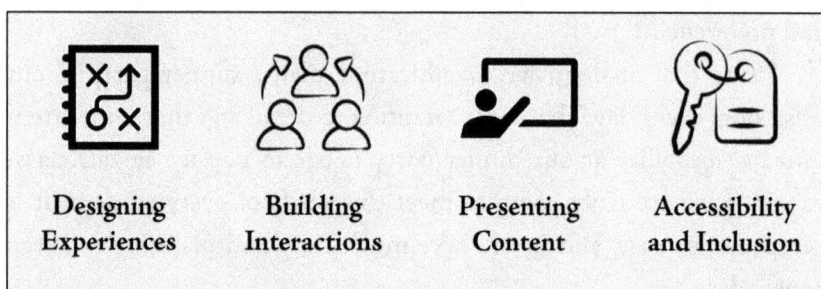

Designing Experiences	Building Interactions	Presenting Content	Accessibility and Inclusion

As educators, we understand that perfecting our craft is an ongoing process. But, with a plethora of educational frameworks, best practices, and teaching strategies, it can be overwhelming to find a starting point. That's where EDI comes in.

EDI is a dynamic approach to teaching and learning that integrates key components from many of the major educational frameworks in use today, and organizes them into four easy-to-understand themes. Each theme offers actionable strategies adaptable to any learning environment, whether teaching in the traditional classroom or in a different setting, EDI gives teachers the tools necessary to maximize student agency and promote inclusivity in their classrooms.

By synthesizing the components of the Future Ready Framework, the principles of Universal Design for Learning (UDL), the stages of Understanding by Design (UbD), and a variety of Differentiated Instruction (DI) practices, EDI ties together these seemingly independent educational approaches. It also incorporates the findings of renowned researchers such as Hattie, Marzano, Borup, and others.

Unlike many books on instructional design, this book stands out by addressing the unique challenges and opportunities presented by online and blended learning during the COVID era. It also offers strategies and tips for designing effective and engaging lessons applicable to any course modalities. Furthermore, this book equips teachers with actionable strategies aligned with the four EDI themes and ready for immediate implementation.

Don't let modern education's challenges hinder your ability to provide the best learning experiences for your students. Let *Effectively Designed Instruction* guide you in crafting more effective and engaging lessons for your traditional, online, or blended classroom. With this book by your side, you can empower your students to reach their full potential and create a lasting, positive impact on their lives.

Embracing the Journey

Even if you're not a movie buff like me, you'll probably remember the end of the movie *Back to the Future*, when Marty McFly (Michael J. Fox) travels thirty years into the future to the year 2015. The last line in the film, as Marty prepares to take off in the flying DeLorean time machine, the eccentric inventor, Doc Brown (Christopher Lloyd) turns to Marty and says, "Where we're going, we don't need roads." This line is often cited as a memorable moment from the film, as it represents the idea that the possibilities of the future are limitless, even beyond the boundaries of technology and infrastructure. It also echoes the film's themes of adventure, discovery, and possibility, suggesting that the journey that Marty and Doc Brown have embarked upon is not just about going back in time, but about embracing new horizons and pushing the limits of what's possible.

When 2015 finally arrived for me, I was in my second year as Garnet Valley's Director of Technology, and it was my job to lead a district team to create an online learning program for students in my district who either needed or wanted a different learning experience than the traditional brick and mortar school. After many months of research and brainstorming sessions, we purchased a canned digital curriculum from a national provider, handed Chromebooks to five students who were to be our virtual school pilot program group, high-fived our team members, and proclaimed that we had just started our own virtual school.

As Thomas Edison famously said, "I have not failed. I've just found 10,000 ways that won't work." Needless to say, we found what doesn't work, as our initial pilot was not well received by our five students or their parents. Who could have known that simply buying a generic, digitalized curriculum and handing out Chromebooks wouldn't suffice? It was 2015, after all.

When combined, our team had hundreds of years of experience in education; we had just gotten to 1:1 (one device per student) and thought that providing a Chromebook to students to learn on their own and at their own pace equated to virtual learning. At that time, we had not fully understood instructional design, we didn't have a learning management system (LMS), and the EDI Framework, which was to become our foundation for teacher training, was not even in place. Little did we know that our journey towards maximizing student agency and inclusivity through intentional instructional design was just beginning.

It was actually through a district-wide committee a year later, I learned we were, in fact, using sixteen different LMS tools in our classrooms. Yes, sixteen different LMS. In one school district. We have since settled on one LMS (Schoology), have moved from Chromebooks to

MacBooks and iPads, and have two virtual schools (eSchool@Garnet-Valley and GVvirtual) that are now flourishing.

As much as a flop our initial virtual school pilot was in 2015, it taught me many things that remain with me today. I learned the importance of being adaptable, that it's OK to not always have the correct answer, and sometimes, in order to know what works, it's best to see what doesn't work. I also discovered the significance of adequately training and supporting our teachers in order to help them effectively make the transition to virtual teaching.

In the absence of a clear vision for the program, our virtual school teachers faced many challenges when trying to provide the same quality education in the online environment as our students experienced in the traditional brick-and-mortar classroom. It was during the ideation of what was to become our virtual program that I was reminded that, whether traditional or not, schools consist of diverse individuals. This was evident to me in the brick-and-mortar setting, but somehow, I overlooked this crucial aspect when creating our online program.

To illustrate this point, when we opened our door to online learners, we had a professional soccer player, a figure skater working towards the Olympics, a student with severe health issues, a student with school phobia, and a student on the verge of dropping out of school. What became clear to me was the following:

Students have many different learning styles. Some students may be visual learners, while others may be auditory learners. Some students may prefer hands-on experiences, while others may prefer more traditional methods of instruction. By considering the diverse learning styles of our students, we are now able to create lessons that are more engaging and more effective for the students in our school district.

Students have different backgrounds and experiences. Students come to the classroom with a wide range of backgrounds and experiences, and it is important to consider these differences when creating lessons. For example, students who have experienced trauma or other challenges may need additional support and accommodations in order to succeed. For this reason, we learned early on to include our special education and support services in just about every decision we make related to instruction.

Students have different goals and interests. Not all students are interested in the same things, and it is important to create lessons that align with the goals and interests of each student in the classroom. By doing so, educators are able to help students feel more motivated and engaged in their learning.

Being reminded that every student learns differently and has different goals and interests allowed my colleagues and me to address the shortcomings of our initial pilot, and create a more inclusive and effective learning environment for our online learners. Although we were proud of the improvements that were made to address the program's flaws, we understood that simply offering classes in different learning formats was insufficient. To genuinely personalize learning for all students, we also needed to transform and personalize the professional development we were providing to our teachers.

> To genuinely personalize learning for all students, we also needed to transform and personalize the professional development we were providing to our teachers.

In the years following our virtual school pilot, including those during the COVID-19 pandemic, I became passionate about intentional instructional design and its role in creating engaging, inclusive learning experiences for students across all learning formats. It's through these learned experiences that led to the development of the strategies and approaches detailed in this book.

~

CHAPTER I

EDI Theme:
Designing Experiences

"We do not remember days, we remember moments."

—Cesare Pavese

Welcome to *Designing Experiences*, a chapter that serves as a compass guiding educators to create immersive, personalized, and innovative learning experiences for their students. As we embark on this exciting journey, let's first take a moment to review our roadmap for this chapter:

EDI Focus	Benefits to Students	Try It Out
Transforming the classroom environment to facilitate experiential learning.	Experiential Learning enhances comprehension and retention of knowledge by enabling students to apply theory to practice.	Key Principles to Consider When Transforming a Classroom (p. 22)

EDI Focus	Benefits to Students	Try It Out
Personalizing instruction through the use of Open Educational Resources (OER).	OER provides tailored learning materials that cater to individual learning styles and paces, and can promote a more inclusive and effective learning environment.	Implementing OER by Using the Three C's Approach to OER (p. 28)
Creating peaks in lessons by leveraging authentic learning.	Authentic learning engages students with real-world issues and problems, and increases motivation and the relevance of their learning.	Four Strategies for Creating Authentic Learning Projects (p. 34)
Using Choice Boards to promote active learning.	Choice Boards encourage student autonomy and decision-making, and can promote critical thinking skills and increasing engagement.	The Ultimate Guide to Using Choice Boards and Learning Menus (p. 42)
Using formative assessments to ensure an 11-star educational experience.	Formative assessments provide continuous feedback to students on their learning, facilitate timely adjustments and improvements to lessons, and can support better learning outcomes for all students.	Using the 3-2-1 Exit Ticket Strategy (p. 45)

EDI Focus	Benefits to Students	Try It Out
Adding exam wrappers to summative assessments to help students develop metacognitive skills.	Exam Wrappers promote self-reflection on learning strategies and habits, and can help students to become more effective and independent learners.	Adding Exam Wrappers to Summative Assessments (p. 49)

Each row in the chart represents a step in our journey. Each step outlines a unique and transformative strategy designed to ignite the power of experiential and active learning. The 'EDI Focus' column outlines the central focus of each section, while the 'Benefits to Students' column illustrates the positive impact each strategy can have on student learning. The "Try It Out" column provides you with a sneak peek of the practical, hands-on tools and tips that await you in each section.

Each section of this chapter unfolds a new narrative of transformation, innovation, and student-centered approaches, backed by practical tools and tips for implementation. As you read, I hope that you will find yourself not only inspired, but also well-equipped to enact these strategies in your own classrooms. Together, let's reimagine the boundaries of what's possible in education, one transformative strategy at a time. Buckle up and get ready for a transformative journey in education that begins now.

Transform the Environment, Transform the Experience

One of the most challenging aspects of teaching World History to 10th grade students is helping them to comprehend the enormity of history-changing events. It's easy for students to assume that events happening overseas don't impact them. It's also understandable when students find it difficult to grasp the importance of events that happened so long ago.

When teaching the events of World War I, I often found myself facing an uphill battle, because students were more interested in the events of World War II and other more recent wars. Perhaps that's Hollywood's influence or the results of video games like *Call of Duty*. Either way, when it came time for me to teach the First World War, I often found myself struggling to motivate my students.

A breakthrough came when a colleague suggested transforming my classroom into trench warfare when teaching this unit. Inspired by this idea, I had students redesign the classroom, using desks as makeshift walls and creating an atmosphere reminiscent of the trenches. As the students took in the transformed space, their eyes widened, their attention focused, signaling to me that they knew they were about to experience something unique and memorable.

To enhance the accuracy of the simulation, I played audio recordings from World War I battles to immerse students in the sounds of the time. Students then participated in a modified dodgeball game, throwing paper balls as ammunition and navigating between the rows of desks to simulate trench warfare. Within minutes, every student in the classroom was immersed in the simulation. Even students who wouldn't normally participate in class were eager to join in the fun.

During the play, I heard one student remark, "This is intense! I've never experienced anything like this in school before." At one point, the lesson turned way too realistic for my taste as a student caught her nose on the edge of a desk as she was ducking for cover. At first, I didn't know what had happened until I saw the blood pour out onto the desks in front of me. Luckily, I had my gym bag close by and was able to grab a towel to stop the blood from splattering all over the other students.

Teachable moment: while the blood-stained rug did provide for a more realistic simulation in the subsequent classes, it's a good idea to provide clarity around your directions and be sure to remind students of your classroom safety procedures.

As the trench warfare simulation progressed, students became frustrated with the stalemate, mirroring the soldiers' experiences during World War I. This frustration led to a deeper understanding of the concept of attrition and the horrific realities of trench warfare. After the simulation, I was able to facilitate a discussion about the students' experiences, asking questions to gauge their understanding of trench warfare and its resulting stalemate. Their insightful responses demonstrated a strong grasp of the concepts and a newfound interest to explore the events of World War I even deeper.

The trench warfare activity remains a memorable learning experience for my former students. When I encounter students even today, they always remember the trench warfare activity. While I don't recommend this modified dodgeball game for younger students, designing immersive, engaging lessons tailored to their students' needs can be applied to any grade level and subject area. For example, a science teacher might simulate a volcanic eruption to teach about natural disasters, while a literature teacher could have students act out scenes from a play to explore themes and character development. By transforming the learning environment, educators can create lasting impressions and help students make meaningful connections with the material.

EDI Strategy: Creating a Classroom Environment That Transforms the Learning Experience

Crafting an effective learning experience often means going beyond traditional teaching methods and creating a classroom environment that fosters active engagement, collaboration, and deeper understanding. This involves not only tailoring lesson plans to students' needs but also transforming the physical space of the classroom to support the learning objectives.

While the prospect of transforming the classroom environment to facilitate active learning might sound daunting, it need not involve drastic or daily changes to the physical setup. Remember, the goal isn't to reconstruct the entire classroom each day, but to adopt small, meaningful strategies that transform the learning experience. Here are several key principles I adhere to when planning and executing a classroom transformation:

> **Align the transformation with learning objectives:** The classroom transformation should be designed to support and enhance the learning objectives of the lesson. Consider how the environment can be adapted to facilitate understanding and provide opportunities for students to apply new knowledge and skills.
>
> **Create an immersive experience:** Design the classroom environment to fully engage students by incorporating relevant materials, props, and visuals. Make use of available technology, such as audio recordings, videos, or interactive simulations, to deepen the immersion and enhance the learning experience.
>
> **Ensure student safety:** Unlike my WWI example, when transforming the classroom, prioritize student safety by establishing clear rules and guidelines for participation. Carefully consider any potential hazards and take necessary precautions to minimize risks. Be prepared to handle emergencies and provide assistance as needed.

Foster collaboration and teamwork: Encourage collaboration and teamwork by assigning roles to students and designing activities that require them to work together. This not only supports social learning but also helps students develop essential communication and problem-solving skills.

Plan for assessment and reflection: Incorporate opportunities for students to reflect on their experiences and demonstrate their understanding of the material. This could include debriefing discussions, written reflections, or assessments that require students to apply their learning to new scenarios.

By following these guidelines when transforming the classroom environment, you can create engaging, memorable learning experiences that resonate with our students and support the goals of our learning objectives.

Take for example, Mrs. Elise Miller, middle school science teacher in Lancaster, Pennsylvania. Mrs. Miller faced a common challenge experienced by many middle school science teachers: how to engage students in learning about space exploration and the science behind it. She knew that simply lecturing about the topic would not be enough to create a lasting impact on her students. Drawing inspiration from the Apollo 13 mission, Mrs. Miller decided to transform her classroom environment to simulate the experience of astronauts and ground control personnel during the historic space mission.

Mrs. Miller divided her class into two groups: astronauts aboard the Apollo 13 spacecraft and the mission control team on Earth. She rearranged the classroom furniture to create separate areas for each group, setting up a "mission control" area complete with computers, headsets, and a large screen displaying mission data. The "lunar module" area was created using tables, chairs, and props to simulate the confined space of the Apollo 13 capsule.

During the simulation, the students in the "lunar module" faced a series of challenges, such as equipment malfunctions and limited resources which mirrored the real-life difficulties faced by the Apollo 13 astronauts. They also had to communicate with their peers in "mission control" to find solutions to these problems and ensure a safe return to Earth. To make the experience even more authentic, Mrs. Miller provided the students with actual transcripts and audio recordings from the Apollo 13 mission. She also assigned roles to each student, such as flight director, spacecraft communicator, and guidance officer, allowing them to take ownership of their tasks and work together as a team.

After completing the simulation, the students debriefed as a class, discussing the challenges they faced, the solutions they developed, and the teamwork required to overcome the obstacles. Mrs. Miller assessed their understanding of space exploration and the science behind it by asking questions and having students reflect on their experiences in a written assignment.

The Apollo 13 simulation left a lasting impression on the students, it also helped them comprehend the complexities of space exploration and the importance of teamwork in problem-solving. By transforming the classroom environment, Mrs. Miller was able to create an engaging, immersive learning experience that resonated with her students and sparked their interest in the topic.

Learning from Disney's Imagineering Team

Have you ever taken a cruise? If so, you probably know that inside staterooms are considered less desirable due to their lack of windows or balconies. This often leads to lower occupancy rates and less revenue for cruise lines. Recognizing this issue, Disney sought to find a way to make the interior rooms not only more appealing but also provide a unique and unforgettable experience for their guests.

As the company planned their cruise line, they focused on providing an exceptional experience for every guest on board, regardless of the type of stateroom they booked. The Disney Imagineering team was tasked with finding a solution that would allow all passengers to enjoy an ocean view, even those in the inner cabins.

Their creative solution was the development of the Magical Porthole, a 42-inch LED monitor that provides a real-time view of the outside, corresponding to the stateroom's location on the ship. By using high-definition cameras mounted around the ship, Disney was able to deliver an authentic, real-time view of the ocean to guests in the interior staterooms. This innovative approach not only addressed the issue of limited natural light and views in inside cabins but also added a unique and magical touch that distinguished Disney Cruise Line from its competitors.

To further enhance the guest experience and stay true to Disney's commitment to storytelling, the company incorporated animated snippets that overlay the actual view from the Magical Porthole. These brief, unexpected animations feature beloved Disney characters and are designed to surprise and delight guests by adding an element of fun and wonder to their stay. This creative addition is reminiscent of other Disney attractions and highlights the company's dedication to bringing magic and imagination to all aspects of their offerings.

Disney's decision to add magical portholes to the inner cabins on their cruise ships was driven by a desire to address a longstanding challenge in the cruise industry and to ensure that all guests, regardless of their stateroom type, could enjoy an unforgettable experience. This innovative solution not only made the interior rooms more desirable but also demonstrated Disney's commitment to creativity, guest satisfaction, and their unique brand of storytelling. The magical portholes serve as a powerful example of how a creative and guest-centric approach can transform challenges into opportunities and create memorable experiences that set a company apart from its competition.

In the same way Disney used innovation and creativity to enhance the experience of their cruise line guests, we too can learn from this example and apply it to our own classrooms. Designing engaging experiences for students is an essential component of education today, as it not only makes learning more enjoyable but also helps students retain information more effectively.

The story of the magical portholes demonstrates the importance of addressing challenges and turning them into opportunities. In the context of a classroom, teachers may face limitations such as limited resources, overcrowded classrooms, and even student apathy towards school. By adopting a creative problem-solving mindset, like the one displayed by the Disney Imagineering team, teachers can transform these limitations into unique and engaging learning experiences for their students.

One of the best examples of this comes from Mr. Jose Rojas, a high school World Language teacher in Wilmington, Delaware. Mr. Rojas teaches a number of students who come from economically disadvantaged households. He knows getting them motivated to learn about a foreign country isn't the easiest thing to do since many of his students may never have the opportunity to travel abroad. Just like Disney found a way to make the inside staterooms more desirable by blending reality with animation, Mr. Rojas decided to incorporate virtual reality (VR) field trips into his high school World Language classroom.

By adding VR into his lessons, Mr. Rojas was able to *Effectively Design Instruction* and create a richer and more dynamic learning experience that captures students' attention and imagination. Using the VR headsets and software, Mr. Rojas is able to transport his students to different parts of the world, giving them a firsthand experience of the culture, people, and language they learn about in his class. The impact on his students was immediate and profound. They were engaged, excited, and eager to explore new places and learn about new cultures. They were no longer passive learners but active participants in their own education. They asked questions, made connections, and shared their own experiences and perspectives.

One student in particular, Miguel, benefitted using VR to travel across the globe. Prior to using VR, Miguel was easily distracted and disengaged in class. He often seemed bored and uninterested, and he struggled to see the relevance of the subject matter to his own life and experiences. However, when Mr. Rojas introduced VR to the class, Miguel's behavior and attitude towards learning changed dramatically. He was able to see and experience different parts of the world and cultures in a way that felt real and relevant to him.

For example, during a lesson about Spain, Miguel was able to virtually walk through the Great Mosque of Cordoba and explore the beautiful Islamic art. He was amazed by the history and architecture and was able to connect the dots between what he was learning in class and the world he saw around him outside of school. As a result of these experiences, Miguel became much more engaged and focused in class. He no longer saw the subject matter as irrelevant, and he started to participate more actively in discussions and activities. His grades improved significantly, and he even started to ask questions and offer his own ideas and perspectives in other lessons.

Virtual reality played a significant role in Miguel's transformation. It allowed him to see the world in a way that was both immersive and accessible, and it gave him a sense of relevance and connection that was missing from traditional classroom methods. For the students who may not have the opportunity to travel, VR can be a window into the world. It can broaden horizons, expand understanding of different cultures, and foster empathy and respect for diversity. By addressing challenges, incorporating elements of surprise, and creating immersive and interactive environments, Mr. Rojas is able to design engaging and meaningful experiences for his students, just as Disney has done for its cruise line guests.

For educators who might not have access to immersive technologies like Virtual Reality in their classrooms but still aspire to enhance engagement and personalize the learning journey for their students, I've found leveraging Open Educational Resources (OER) has proven to be a remarkably effective way to inspire a sense of relevance and connection in students.

OER is freely accessible, openly licensed text, media, and other digital media that teachers can add to their teaching toolkit. Depending on the type of license, many OER resources allow teachers to adapt, modify, and align materials to meet individual learning needs and styles. I can't think of a better way to create opportunities for more dynamic, personalized, and learner-centered teaching practices than to ditch the textbook and bring OER into your classroom.

EDI Strategy: Using OER to Create Your Own Magic Portholes

The use of Open Educational Resources (OER) is becoming increasingly popular in K-12 education due to its overall cost savings and potential to revolutionize how learning materials are brought into the education system. However, it's been my experience that the real excitement for teachers comes from the ability to personalize the learning experience for their students.

Just as Disney's Imagineering Team used magical portholes to transform the cruise experience, many teachers are leveraging OER to provide "windows, mirrors, and sliding glass doors" for students. By doing so, teachers provide resources that celebrate the histories, experiences, and everyday life of the students they serve. Just as VR did for Mr. Rojas' class, OER allows teachers to promote cross-cultural understanding, empathy, and a sense of global citizenship.

"Windows" refers to experiences that open up new perspectives and cultures to students, allowing them to broaden their understanding of the world and the people in it. "Mirrors" refers to experiences that reflect the lives and experiences of the students themselves, allowing them to see themselves in what they are learning and making the content more relevant and meaningful to them. "Sliding Glass Doors" refers to experiences that allow students to move back and forth between the perspectives they have learned, to understand the connection between their own experiences and those of others, and to develop a sense of empathy and perspective-taking.

The benefits of using openly licensed resources are that it helps to create a more inclusive and culturally responsive education that better meets the needs and experiences of all students, regardless of their background. It also helps to promote cross-cultural understanding, empathy, and a sense of global citizenship. Even for an OER enthusiast like me, finding OER can sometimes be intimidating, and for teachers new to it, it can be frustrating since there is no single repository of resources.

Under the leadership of our former Curriculum Supervisor, Anthony Gabriele, Garnet Valley joined the #GoOpen Movement in 2016 and quickly became an exemplar school district in this area. To provide our teachers with an effective way to personalize the learning experience for students using OER, we developed the 3C's approach to OER: Collecting, Curating, and Creating.

Collect. Gather existing resources from colleagues, determine their status related to appropriate use and complete an inventory to use in lesson design.

Curate: Find and vet online resources that fit the learning objectives identified in the curriculum documents.

Create: New resources to fill gaps in the resource inventory.

Our 3C's approach to OER has become more flexible and less daunting for teachers as we have refined it over time by working with teachers in Garnet Valley and others, in addition to partnering with *Edvative Learning.*

One success story comes from Dr. Robin Worley, Educational Specialist and Online Curriculum Developer for the Hawaii Department of Education's State Distance Learning Program (SDLP). During many conversations, Dr. Worley expressed her frustration with the limited number of resources available to effectively teach students in her state. From her perspective, it was like the entire textbook publishing and digital content industry skipped over Hawaii when creating school resources. Despite her best efforts, and those of her colleagues, no published content adequately represented their students, prioritized their diversity, or honored their culture.

As a result, Dr. Worley and her team partnered with *Edvative Learning* and accepted the challenge of personalized learning so that her teachers could *Effectively Design Instruction* and build a curriculum that represented their student population. By working with our amazing Instructional Design Coaches, SDLP teachers were able to collect, curate, and create OER resources that prioritized their student's diversity and honored their student's culture.

Designing Experiences Using the Peak-End Rule

What if you could transform your classroom into a place where students of all abilities are excited to learn and eager to participate? It's not impossible. In fact, this was my experience while visiting Mr. Zimmerman's Physics class at Westfield High School (Westfield, Indiana). This co-taught Physics class brought together regular and special education students of mixed grades and academic abilities. And despite the students' initial lack of interest in Physics, every student in this class eventually claimed it to be their favorite.

Searching for ways to make his Physics class more engaging and inclusive, Mr. Zimmerman stumbled upon an article on the Peak-End Rule, a cognitive bias affecting how people remember past events. The principles of the Peak-End Rule suggest that people tend to remember past events based on two key moments: the peak of the experience and the end of the experience.

Before learning about the Peak-End Rule, Mr. Zimmerman's lessons followed the traditional format: lectures, textbook readings, problem-solving exercises, and occasional lab work. However, many students struggled to maintain interest and see the relevance of Physics to their everyday lives. To design more inclusive and engaging learning experiences, Mr. Zimmerman decided to implement the Peak-End Rule in his lesson plans.

> People tend to remember past events based on two key moments: the peak of the experience and the end of the experience.

By incorporating different teaching strategies and activities that resonated with his diverse group of students, Mr. Zimmerman was able to create peaks in the learning experience that left a lasting impression. Additionally, he made sure to end each class on a positive note, whether it was through a fun activity or by highlighting the progress the class had made that day. By doing so, he ensured that his students would remember the class positively, leading to increased motivation and engagement in future classes.

In a lesson on gravity and free fall, Mr. Zimmerman started with a captivating demonstration, dropping a bowling ball and a small rubber ball from the same height at the same time. The students were amazed when both hit the ground simultaneously, creating a "peak" experience that immediately "piqued" their interest. He then divided the students into small groups for a hands-on activity that allowed them to explore the concept further. One by one, students began dropping various objects from different heights.

As the lesson drew to a close, Mr. Zimmerman shared a video of astronauts conducting a similar experiment on the moon, reinforcing his students' understanding of gravity and free fall in a memorable and engaging way. As a final touch, he handed each student a small rubber ball to use for a homework assignment that night. Each ball had the handwritten message "have fun and shoot for the stars," which created an obvious connection to the lesson that had just occurred in class, as well as creating a positive "end" to the activity.

By incorporating the Peak-End Rule into his teaching, Mr. Zimmerman successfully designed learning experiences that maximized student agency and inclusivity, and transformed his Physics classroom into an engaging, interactive, and memorable environment. Students who previously had no interest in the subject now found themselves excited about Physics and motivated to continue learning.

As educators, we can learn from Mr. Zimmerman's innovative approach and consider how we might implement the Peak-End Rule in our own classrooms. By intentionally designing engaging and inclusive learning experiences, we can not only improve students' performance but also foster a love for learning and a passion for discovering the world around them. In the next section, we will explore practical tips and strategies for implementing the Peak-End Rule and designing memorable, authentic learning experiences for all students.

☀ EDI Strategy: Create Peaks in Your Lessons by Leveraging Authentic Learning

Authentic learning is a powerful instructional approach that encourages students to apply their knowledge to real-world situations and challenges. This strategy is crucial in preparing students for a future in which they must navigate a complex world with creativity and resilience. It's been my experience that engaging students in real-world projects and problem-solving activities is one of the most effective ways to prepare them for their futures.

Technology has certainly made it easier to implement authentic learning projects in schools today. For instance, community service initiatives like the United Nations Sustainable Goals Project allow students to collaborate with local or global organizations to address a number of pressing issues. Social studies teachers can have students research historical events or individuals and present their findings through written reports, podcasts, or videos. Science teachers can ask students to design and conduct experiments, such as investigating the impact of plastic waste on ocean life. These examples demonstrate the diverse range of authentic learning projects that can engage students and connect their learning to real-world contexts.

A common misconception for some educators is that authentic learning projects are only suitable for high-achieving students capable

> Authentic learning projects can be designed to accommodate all students, regardless of their academic abilities or learning needs.

of handling complex tasks. However, like Mr. Zimmerman's Physics class, authentic learning projects can be designed to accommodate all students, regardless of their academic abilities or learning needs. By providing an inclusive, engaging, and real-world learning experience, authentic learning prepares students for a future in which they can thrive, adapt, and contribute to a rapidly changing world.

Here are four strategies I have found effective when working with teachers to create authentic learning projects for their students:

Connect to real-world issues. Design projects that address real-world problems or situations that students can relate to or find meaningful. This will not only engage students but also help them understand the relevance of their learning.

Encourage collaboration. Authentic learning projects often require students to work together in teams which can enhance collaboration and communication skills. Group work also allows students to learn from each other, share ideas, and develop their ability to negotiate and compromise—important skills that will serve them in their future career choices.

Integrate multiple subject areas. When possible, design interdisciplinary projects that require students to draw on knowledge and skills from multiple subject areas. This approach encourages students to make connections between different subjects and helps them see the bigger picture in their learning.

Foster a growth mindset. Encourage students to embrace challenges, learn from setbacks, and view effort as a path to mastery. By promoting a growth mindset, we can help students develop resilience and a lifelong love for learning.

Creating authentic learning projects for students involves designing experiences that allow them to apply their knowledge and skills to real-world situations. These projects not only deepen understanding but also help students develop problem-solving, critical thinking, collaboration, and communication skills.

One powerful example of the impact of authentic learning is demonstrated by an English Language Learner in the Austin Independent School District (Austin, Texas). Lucía, a 10th-grade English Language Learner, struggled with speaking and writing in English. Despite her best efforts, she found it difficult to express herself in a language that wasn't her native language. As a result, she often felt frustrated and discouraged in her English classes.

Despite struggling in class, Lucía was encouraged by her teacher to participate in an authentic learning project to write and perform a poem or short story in English that reflected her experiences and cultural heritage. While initially hesitant, the process of writing and performing a poem in English was empowering, and Lucía's classmates were in awe of the depth and beauty of her words. The poem below was submitted by Lucía as part of an authentic learning challenge organized by *Edvative Learning*.

A Journey Through Unspoken Words

In the classrooms of unfamiliar tongues,
A stranger I was, lost and afraid,
Words swirling around like a river's fierce dance,
I, a leaf adrift, longing for a glade.

The echoes of laughter, distant and cold,
As I fumbled and stumbled with each spoken phrase,
Feeling the weight of unspoken thoughts,
Invisible, yearning for a comforting gaze.

My heart ached with the burden of silence,
A longing for understanding, a guiding hand,
But in the darkness of my struggles,
A flicker of hope began to withstand.

With a pen in hand, I etched my journey,
A testament to the battles I've faced,
A canvas that mirrors my resilience,
The strength of my spirit, in every word traced.

In the verses of my struggles, I found solace,
A sanctuary where my voice rings true,
And as I share my tale in this foreign tongue,
The shadows of my fears slowly undo.

For in this dance of words and rhythm,
I find the courage to stand tall and be heard,
To embrace the beauty of my diversity,
And let my voice soar, like a free, untethered bird.

Now, as I stand before my peers,
My heart swells with pride, and I say,
I am Lucía, a warrior of two worlds,
With the power of language lighting my way.

Although Lucía's poem earned her a second-place finish in her category, the impact of her words extended beyond the competition. Her
writing was truly inspiring for everyone involved in the project. Every
time I read her words, I am filled with admiration and appreciation for
the cultural background that she so beautifully conveyed. Through this
experience, Lucía was able to recognize the value of her heritage and
develop a sense of confidence and comfort in her own learning journey.

Lucía's experience is a powerful example of how authentic learning can make a difference in the life of an English Language Learner and others who may not be considered a traditional student. By providing opportunities for students to connect their learning to their personal experiences and interests, we can help them see the relevance and value of their education.

Empowering Students Through Active Learning

Picture a vibrant classroom where students engage in various learning activities, select tasks based on their learning styles, and decide how to demonstrate their understanding. This dynamic learning environment results from intentional instructional design. By incorporating open-ended, real-world tasks that enable students to make choices and assess their progress, they become active participants in their education. While it's crucial to offer guidance and support, allowing students to take charge of their learning fosters critical thinking, problem-solving, self-reflection, and a sense of belonging.

In one of his blog posts, A.J. Juliani, a renowned author of several educational books, including *Empower: What Happens When Students Own Their Learning*, discusses a 2019 study conducted by Louis Deslauriers. The study aimed to compare the impact of active versus passive instructional strategies on learning outcomes. According to the study, active instructional strategies involved methods such as collaborative problem-solving, peer instruction, and small-group discussions. In this approach, the teacher acted as a facilitator and encouraged students to think critically, work collaboratively, and provided guidance and feedback when needed.

On the other hand, passive instructional strategies were centered around traditional lecturing as a way of delivering course content. Students were expected to listen, take notes, and absorb information presented by the teacher with little interaction or engagement. The study aimed to highlight the effectiveness of active instructional strategies in promoting student engagement, participation, and overall learning outcomes compared to the passive method.

Deslauriers' study showed that despite having significantly higher learning gains than the passive group, students in the active learning group *believed* that they learned less than those in the lecture-style setting. How can this be? Well, this discrepancy between the students' *perceptions* and the *actual* learning gains can be attributed to various factors.

One possible reason is that active learning requires more effort from students, as they engage in problem-solving, discussions, and other interactive activities. This increased effort may make learning feel more challenging, leading students to believe they have learned less than they actually have. In contrast, in a passive learning setting, students might feel like they are absorbing more information as they listen to lectures, even though their actual learning gains may be lower.

Another reason for this perception gap could be students' familiarity with traditional teaching methods. Many students, especially at the secondary level, have become accustomed to traditional lecture-style teaching methods, where the instructor provides information, and students passively absorb it. As a result, they might associate learning with this familiar format and underestimate the effectiveness of active learning activities.

To bridge this gap, it is essential for educators to address these perceptions and help students (and parents) understand the benefits of active learning activities. By doing so, they can help students develop a more accurate and positive perception of their learning experiences and increase engagement, participation, and overall learning outcomes.

There are a few ways I find helpful to address students' perceptions of active learning and help them to understand the benefits of these techniques for their long-term success:

Communicate the benefits. Explicitly discuss the advantages of active learning techniques with students and parents, including improved learning outcomes, better retention of information, and the development of critical thinking skills. Share research findings and real-life examples to help students understand the value of active learning.

Scaffold the transition. If students are not used to active learning techniques, gradually introduce them to these methods. Start with simpler activities and gradually increase the level of challenge and interaction. This can help students become more comfortable and confident with active learning over time.

Set clear expectations. At the beginning of the course or lesson, clearly explain the active learning methods that will be used and the rationale behind them. Establish expectations for participation, collaboration, and engagement, so students understand their role in the learning process.

Encourage self-reflection. Incorporate opportunities for self-assessment and reflection into the learning process. Ask students to evaluate their understanding of the material, identify areas for improvement, and set goals for future learning. This can help students develop metacognitive skills and become more aware of their learning gains.

By addressing students' perceptions of active learning and implementing these strategies, we can help learners understand the benefits of this approach: increased engagement and improved learning outcomes.

EDI Strategy: Using Choice Boards to Promote Active Learning

Choice Boards are an effective tool that can foster student autonomy and promote greater active learning in the classroom. When implemented thoughtfully, Choice Boards empower students to make decisions about their learning by offering a range of options to select from. This approach allows students to take ownership of their learning journey and become more invested in the process.

> Choice Boards are instructional tools that provide students with a variety of options for learning activities related to a specific subject or topic. Presented in a grid or menu format, Choice Boards empower students to choose from a range of tasks or challenges that align with their interests, learning styles, or ability levels. Each option on the board represents a different way to engage with the content, allowing students to take ownership of their learning and explore the material in a way that resonates with them.

These can be customized to include various types of activities, such as reading assignments, videos, hands-on projects, or interactive online tasks. By offering diverse options, these activities foster autonomy, encourage critical thinking, and promote differentiation in the classroom. Choice Boards also encourage students to evaluate options and make informed decisions based on their individual learning needs and interests, which, in turn, enhances critical thinking and problem-solving skills crucial for lifelong learning.

These student-centered activities can be employed to differentiate instruction by presenting options tailored to various levels of understanding. This ensures that all students can work at their own pace and engage with tasks that match their ability level. Additionally, Choice

Boards can be customized to accommodate diverse learning styles and abilities. For instance, options catering to visual learners may include videos or infographics, while kinesthetic learners can benefit from options featuring hands-on activities.

The flexibility and versatility of Choice Boards proved to be invaluable during the pandemic, as they helped teachers facilitate student engagement, autonomy, and inclusivity. These tools provided personalized learning experiences and enabled differentiation within virtual classrooms, offering teachers new to online instruction an effective way to ensure all students had access to meaningful and engaging learning opportunities.

During the pandemic, students confronted a unique set of challenges, including limited social interactions, distractions, and the need for self-motivation. Choice Boards offered an efficient solution for teachers to support their students and maintain a sense of connection despite physical distance. By providing a variety of options, Choice Boards allow students to take ownership of their virtual learning experiences and cater to their own individual needs, interests, and learning styles. This autonomy not only empowered students to take charge of their education, but also helped sustain their motivation amidst unprecedented challenges.

Choice Boards proved to be an effective means of personalization in remote learning environments. As teachers grappled with gauging student progress and providing individualized support in a virtual setting, Choice Boards enabled them to accommodate different ability levels and ensure that all students had access to meaningful and engaging learning experiences. This inclusivity was especially crucial during the pandemic, as students encountered varying degrees of disruption to their learning based on their access to technology, support at home, and personal circumstances.

A.J. Juliani, in his piece, *The Ultimate Guide to Using Choice Boards and Learning Menus*, offers ten insightful recommendations for creating effective Choice Boards to promote active learning. He outlines the process from identifying a concept or skill to allowing for reflection during each activity. AJ highlights the importance of acting as a guide and expert learner rather than merely managing the activity. Take a moment to read through these tips and give Choice Boards a try in your own classrooms.

1. Identify a unit/concept or skill and what you want students to know/do/make in order to demonstrate their understanding/proficiency.
2. Create or choose an assessment/performance task that allows students to demonstrate mastery.
3. List various instructional methods, resources, and strategies to prepare students for the assessment/performance task.
4. Choose four-six instructional methods to turn into choice-board activities. Each activity should be a similar length in time and cover common material. Here is where you can add different types of technology or hands-on experiences to the learning process.
5. Create a workflow for the students to follow. Have notes and formative checks as part of the choice-board design process. Allow for reflection during each activity when planning how long students will complete the activity.
6. Introduce the different choices to students and describe what the goals of the activity are (as well as the assessment this is leading up to).
7. Let students pick activities based on their interests/needs.
8. As the teacher, a few of the activities/options might need more guidance than others. Make sure you aren't just "managing" this activity, but instead truly acting as a guide and expert learner when the opportunity is available.
9. Once the choice-board activities are complete, put students into small groups to "jigsaw" their reflection. Bring students from different activities together to reflect on their learning experience and share (this can be written, audio, or video reflections–think Flipgrid).
10. Listen to reflections and check the formative pieces for each activity to see if students are prepared for the assessment. If not, feel free to go through one more activity together as a class or talk about any topics/concepts they did not understand during the activity.

As education continues to evolve and adapt to the post-pandemic world, the lessons learned from this challenging period, including the value of Choice Boards, will remain relevant in helping teachers *Effectively Design Instruction* and maximize student success, regardless of the educational setting.

For some, Choice Boards may seem more elementary school focused; for others, they provide too much freedom for students. Matt Miller, in his blog on Progressive Choice Boards, provides strategies for such concerns. He discusses the potential overload of too much choice and suggests introducing options to students progressively. His approach enables teachers at all levels to stimulate creativity, empower students, and assist them in making informed decisions about their learning.

As we navigate the post-pandemic educational landscape, the lessons we've gleaned, including the value of Choice Boards, will continue to resonate. They are instrumental in *Effectively Designed Instruction* and can help teachers in all grade levels to maximize student success across different educational settings.

Design an 11-Star Learning Experience for Your Students

Airbnb's "11-star experience" is a concept that emerged from a brainstorming exercise by the company's co-founder, Brian Chesky. The idea was to imagine the best possible experience a guest could have while using Airbnb, going far beyond their expectations. In this exercise, a 5-star experience is considered a basic, satisfactory stay, while an 11-star experience is something extraordinary and unforgettable.

The concept of the 11-star experience serves as a creative approach for companies to continually improve and provide exceptional experiences for their customers. By envisioning the most extreme and remarkable scenarios, they can identify areas where they can innovate, delight their customers, and set themselves apart from competitors. In essence, the 11-star experience encourages teams to push the boundaries of satisfaction, inspiring them to reimagine their services and constantly strive to exceed the expectations of their clients.

The story of Airbnb traces back to the summer of 2004 in Providence, Rhode Island, when co-founders Brian Chesky and Joe Gebbia first crossed paths while collaborating on a student project at the Rhode Island School of Design. By 2007, both had moved to San Francisco, where they found themselves short on rent money. To address their financial need, they rented out three airbeds in their apartment to designers attending a local conference.

This initial success inspired Chesky and Gebbia to develop a web-based service called Airbed & Breakfast. Although they had to relaunch their business three times, they eventually attracted investors, rebranded as Airbnb, and began to experience unprecedented growth. Today, Airbnb is a powerhouse in the internet business era, growing rapidly year after year, and valued at over $31 billion.

Drawing inspiration from Airbnb's journey and philosophy, we, as educators, can learn valuable lessons in creating exceptional learning experiences that cater to every student's unique needs and interests while empowering them to take charge of their own learning journey. Just as Airbnb refined its business model through multiple iterations, creating an 11-star educational experience for our students will require experimentation and adaptation to the way we design our lessons.

EDI Strategy: Using Formative Assessments to Ensure an 11-Star Educational Experience

Formative assessments play an instrumental role in our classrooms today as they aid our understanding of students' progress and knowledge gaps. Regular feedback mechanisms, like these assessments, not only enable teachers to fine-tune their instruction, but also ensure that students are on a clear path to mastering their material. It's safe to say that no student wants to fail, making formative assessments a critical tool for providing instantaneous feedback on student learning progress. By integrating these assessments into our instructional strategies, we pave the way for a top-notch, 11-star educational experience tailored to every learner's needs.

Consider Ms. Rodriguez, a 4th-grade math teacher from Orlando, Florida. She employs an array of formative assessment strategies, including think-pair-share, exit tickets, and fist-to-five, among others. Furthermore, she administers self-assessment quizzes and exit tickets after each lesson to discern the learning progress of each student. These exit tickets are her window into understanding her students' knowledge gaps.

There's beauty in simplicity, and these exit tickets embody that. Ms. Rodriguez prefers the 3-2-1 exit ticket—a straightforward yet effective way for educators to assess student understanding at the end of a lesson. Students are asked to enumerate:

3 Three things they learned from the lesson

2 Two questions they have about the lesson

1 One thing they still don't understand or need clarification on

As students depart the classroom, teachers can gather these exit tickets and examine the responses. This aids in identifying areas needing additional instruction or clarification for the subsequent lesson and provides invaluable feedback on student understanding.

Ms. Rodriguez utilizes the data collected from exit tickets and other formative assessments to genuinely sculpt an 11-star learning experience for her students. She designs targeted instruction for those who need extra support, while allowing others who've already mastered the material to explore further through enrichment activities. As her students pair up to solve math problems, she encourages them to employ a self-assessment rubric, rating their understanding of each step. This rubric aids in identifying areas that require further practice, supplying Ms. Rodriguez with data to plan future instructions and interventions.

The critical role of formative assessments in helping teachers identify and address knowledge gaps in students' understanding can't be overstated. Incorporating these quick checks for understanding into our teaching practices can be accomplished through various methods. Many educational software packages offer built-in formative assessment systems. However, numerous non-technology-based approaches are also available to assess students' progress. By adopting formative assessments and an iterative approach inspired by Airbnb's journey, we can create an 11-star educational experience that maximizes student agency and inclusivity in our classrooms.

Making Metacognition Matter

You probably don't have to think too hard to find an example of a student struggling with a complex problem in class. I have had my share of students who would throw in the towel when faced with challenging or complex problems. But, with the right metacognitive tools in place, students can break down problems, recognize their learning needs, and ultimately overcome the challenges they face in the classroom.

Metacognition is the awareness and understanding of one's own thought processes, or more simply put, metacognition is "thinking about how one thinks." It involves the ability to monitor, evaluate, and regulate one's own learning and cognitive strategies.

Consider these three students: Jamal, Darren, and Liz. Each believes they are not very good at writing; however, their various metacognitive skills lead them down distinctly different academic paths. When faced with a difficult prompt, Jamal decides to spend extra time on his writing assignment, focusing on the task itself and devising a strategy to overcome it. Darren opts to skip this and future writing assignments, believing he lacks the skills to improve. Liz considers withdrawing from school, attributing her writing struggles to a personal characteristic. All three students believed that they weren't very good writers, but because each had a different level of understanding of their learning needs, each ended up with a distinctly different outcome.

Students acquire metacognitive knowledge from three sources: naive belief systems about learning, feedback from others, and experiences driven by emotions. To help students develop metacognitive awareness and skills, teachers can promote reflection as an important aspect of learning. I have found success in this area by encouraging students to ask questions like "What do I know about this topic?", "What strategies have worked for me in the past?", and "How can I improve my understanding?". Incorporating regular self-assessment, reflection, and goal-setting activities can also foster metacognitive skills and promote student agency.

Despite their reputation, I believe summative assessments are useful for teachers; they not only measure how well their students have mastered the material but, when implemented correctly, help students develop more metacognitive awareness. While I do believe summative assessments have their place in our educational system, I also think it's important to acknowledge that they are not always beneficial. Summative assessments, in many classes, are often used as high-stakes exams that have significant consequences for students, such as determining their final grades or whether they will advance to the next grade level.

Additionally, I've witnessed far too many summative assessments that only focus on content retention and memorization. This can be especially problematic for students who struggle with test-taking or have a learning style that does not align with traditional testing methods. If we are to *Effectively Design Instruction* for our students, we'll need to reimagine how we have students show their learning. We'll also need to rethink how to leverage summative assessments to foster metacognitive skills in our students. One strategy that I have found to accomplish this is to add Exam Wrappers at the end of my summative assessments.

💡 EDI Strategy: Adding Exam Wrappers to Summative Assessments to Help Students Develop Metacognitive Skills

All too often, when students receive back a graded assessment, they focus on a single feature—the score they earned. It's understandable, of course, but this narrow emphasis can cause students to overlook multiple opportunities for learning that the assessment can provide. For this reason, I started using Exam Wrappers after giving summative assessments to help my students reflect on their performance and adjust their study habits to benefit future learning.

Exam wrappers are one-page handouts that prompt students to review their performance and use that information to inform their future studies. This allows students to identify their strengths and weaknesses, reflect on their preparation and study methods, and recognize recurring patterns in their errors that need addressing. Exam wrappers can be repeated throughout the school year to help students adjust their study habits and strategies as needed.

Utilizing Exam Wrappers, teachers can *Effectively Design Instruction* by focusing on executive functioning and higher-order thinking skills. Inviting students to contemplate their preparation for an assignment/exam, what transpired well, what didn't, and potential changes in future study habits offers a chance to reflect, compare, and adjust their learning habits and strategies. To effectively implement Exam Wrappers, I suggest the following guidelines:

➡ Ensure the Exam Wrappers are focused on the study/metacognitive skills you want to promote.

➡ Ensure the Exam Wrappers are flexible enough to add minor adaptations for each assignment.

➡ Ensure the Exam Wrappers are short enough to complete relatively quickly (10 minutes or less).

➡ Ensure the Exam Wrappers are non-graded or graded based on completion only.

Given that summative assessments are typically conducted at the end of a unit or semester, they may not always offer timely feedback that students can leverage to improve their understanding of the material. For this reason, I advocate for the use of Exam Wrappers, as they provide students with opportunities to reflect on their learning and develop the essential metacognitive skills needed to overcome challenging situations. Feel free to repurpose the two Exam Wrappers below and be sure to check out the Free Resources section on the *Edvative Learning* website (www.edvative.com) to access even more styles of Exam Wrappers.

DESIGNING EXPERIENCES
Elementary
Assessment Wrapper

Name _____   **Topic** _____

How I feel about this assessment or assignment.

I studied for the assessment by:

- ☐ Checking my flashcards
- ☐ Asking someone to quiz me
- ☐ Reading my text
- ☐ Other

The assessment was hard because:

- ☐ There were words I didn't understand
- ☐ There were questions I wasn't sure about
- ☐ I ran out of time
- ☐ Other

During the assessment, I used these strategies to help me:

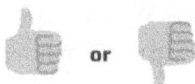

👍 or 👎   👍 or 👎   👍 or 👎

Underlined Key Words   Drew pictures   Re-read Questions

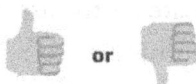

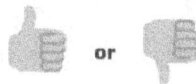

My goals for my next assessment are:

- ☐ Get a higher grade
- ☐ Finish the assessment on time
- ☐ Understand the assessment better
- ☐ Other

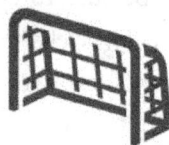

I will achieve my goals by:

- ☐ Asking my teacher for help.
- ☐ Practicing different strategies.
- ☐ Studying with a friend.
- ☐ Other

DESIGNING EXPERIENCES

Secondary
Exam Wrapper

Name		Score	
Exam		Grade	

Time Invested

How much time did I spend studying for this exam?	
When did I start studying for this exam?	
Do I feel that was enough time?	

Reviewing the test or assignment, where did I lose points & why?

☐ Not answering a question.
☐ Not reading a question carefully.
☐ Not knowing the content.
☐ Careless mistake.
☐ Exam conditions.
☐ Not applying the skills the way they should have been.

What Questions Did I Find Most Challenging?
1.
2.
3.
4.
5.

What percentage of studying did I do for this exam?

Percentage of time that I spent on each activity to prepare for this exam.

☐	Read assigned readings in text.	☐	Studied with a friend.
☐	Attended before/after study sessions.	☐	Met with teacher for 1 on 1 support.
☐	Reviewed notes.	☐	Other.

Moving Forward

Three things I will do differently for the next exam or assignment

1.
2.
3.

Reflecting on Designing Experiences

In this chapter, we journeyed through six pivotal areas that educators should consider to craft engaging and potent learning experiences for their students. We drew attention to the need to cultivate a nurturing classroom atmosphere, a safe space where learners can freely communicate, collaborate, and hone critical skills. The significance of forming effective cooperative learning groups, setting clear expectations, and facilitating positive and productive peer interactions were underlined.

We spotlighted the utility of Open Educational Resources (OER), instrumental tools that empower teachers to customize learning experiences, celebrate student diversity, and foster empathy within the classroom. The vital role of authentic learning was emphasized, connecting students to real-world issues and contexts, thereby enabling them to explore, discuss, and form meaningful associations between concepts.

Key elements of Project-Based Learning (PBL) were illuminated, providing students with a clear purpose that fuels their learning as they undertake projects rooted in their interests and real-world relevance. Lastly, the crucial balance between formative and summative assessments was underscored. Frequent feedback, which helps students understand their learning needs, allows them to spot knowledge gaps and amend their study habits accordingly.

Employing the strategies detailed in this chapter, teachers can fashion a more inclusive, captivating, and effective learning environment, guiding their students towards success. As you reflect on the information shared in this chapter, contemplate the following questions:

1. With insights from the trench warfare simulation, what key takeaways or ideas might you harness to transform your classroom space?

2. What measures can you undertake to construct "magical port-holes" for your students, turning challenges or limitations into extraordinary learning prospects?

3. How can you employ the principles of the Peak-End Rule to design memorable and inclusive student experiences, akin to what Mr. Zimmerman achieved with his Physics class?

4. In what ways can you integrate the recommendations from AJ Juliani, and others to develop effective Choice Boards that cater to diverse student abilities?

5. How can you leverage formative assessment data, mirroring Ms. Rodriguez's approach with her 4th graders, to create an 11-star learning experience?

6. How might you incorporate Exam Wrappers into your summative assessments to facilitate opportunities for students to reflect on their learning journey?

~

CHAPTER II

EDI Theme: Building Interactions

"The most meaningful learning occurs when students are actively engaged in the learning process, whether through discussion, collaboration, or hands-on activities. When students are able to interact with each other and their teacher, they are able to ask questions, clarify their understanding, and share their own ideas, leading to a deeper and more lasting understanding of the material."

–John Dewey

Imagine a classroom buzzing with engaged students, eagerly participating in meaningful discussions and collaborating on intriguing projects. This ideal learning environment is within reach, and the key to unlocking it lies in the next critical element: Building Interactions.

The Building Interactions theme explores the importance of creating meaningful student connections in the classroom. These connections not only promote student agency and inclusivity, but they also keep students actively involved in their learning journey. Research has shown that students learn and retain more when actively engaged in the learning process. However, if you are like me and so many other educators today, sometimes it can be challenging to maintain student engagement throughout an entire lesson or unit of study.

As we embark on learning more about this critical topic, let's first take a moment to review our roadmap for this chapter:

EDI Focus	Benefits to Students	Try It Out
Addressing the struggle for engagement with student-to-student feedback.	Student-to-student Feedback facilitates active learning and fosters critical thinking as students have the chance to review and critique each other's work.	20-Minute Peer Feedback Activity (p. 64).
Fostering a culture of continuous improvement and reflection through Student-to-Teacher Feedback.	By actively seeking student feedback, educators can continuously refine their teaching strategies and methodologies to better meet their students' needs.	Tips for using student-to-teacher surveys (p. 71).
Leveraging class discussions to get students to ask more questions.	Class discussions help develop communication skills, critical thinking, and confidence, as students are required to articulate their thoughts and defend their ideas.	Planning for Class Discussions (p. 75).

EDI Focus	Benefits to Students	Try It Out
Using reflective journaling as an asynchronous activity.	Reflective journaling provides students with an opportunity to analyze their learning and encourages them to articulate their thoughts, insights, and questions.	Prompts to encourage students to think deeply about their learning (p. 81).
Providing positive teacher-to-student feedback to build and enhance connections.	Positive feedback can greatly improve a student's confidence and motivation, leading to a more engaged and enthusiastic learner.	Moving from feedback to feedforward (p. 84).
Creating collaborative learning opportunities to foster interdependence.	Collaborative learning fosters a sense of community among students, boosts communication skills, and can lead to improved problem-solving capabilities.	Mitigate the risk of "freeriding" during group activities (p. 90).

This theme presents an array of strategies designed to effectively engage students through feedback, asynchronous and synchronous activities, and collaborative learning experiences. By embracing the strategies outlined in this chapter, you can transform your classroom into a space that promotes meaningful interactions and encourages active student participation in the learning process. So, let's dive into Building Interactions and unlock the full potential of your instructional practice.

The Struggle for Engagement

During the peak of the pandemic, Mrs. Thompson, a devoted English teacher from Lakewood City School District (Cleveland, Ohio) faced the challenge of keeping her students engaged in remote learning. She observed that distractions, lack of structure, and social isolation were taking a toll on her students' motivation and focus. Like her colleagues in the Interboro School District mentioned earlier in the book, the pandemic forced Mrs. Thompson to double her determination to explore new, innovative, student-centered approaches to learning that would rekindle her students' engagement and unleash their full potential while learning remotely.

To tackle the challenges faced by Mrs. Thompson and countless others during the pandemic, we must first understand the three pillars of student engagement as outlined by Teachers' College at Columbia University:

Academic engagement refers to students' ability to complete academic tasks.

Intellectual engagement involves activating students' interests, gifts, and talents.

Social-emotional engagement encompasses the connections students make while in school.

The shift to online learning during the pandemic presented many challenges for educators and students alike. One of the most significant was how to address the struggle many students had to stay motivated and focused. My guess is that your district, like mine, saw many factors contributing to the lack of student engagement. Some of these factors included:

Distractions at home: For many students, learning from home meant navigating a range of distractions, from siblings and pets to household chores and household stress. These distractions made it difficult for students to focus on their studies.

Lack of structure: The structure and routine of a traditional classroom can be a powerful motivator for students. Without this structure, many students struggled to stay on track and complete assignments on time.

Technology issues: Many students encountered technical issues that prevented them from participating fully in online learning. For students in our district, this was frustrating and demotivating.

Social isolation: The dramatic shift to online learning was isolating for students, especially for those who already struggled with social anxiety or other mental health issues. This isolation made it difficult for students to feel connected to their peers and to their learning.

While the COVID-19 pandemic shone a spotlight on student engagement, it's important to acknowledge that these issues have always existed in our schools. Dr. Roberta Lenger Kang, Director at Teachers College, Columbia University, aptly stated:

COVID hasn't given us any problems we didn't already have. So, our challenge is to redesign what engagement looks like, what it feels like, and what it takes to get kids onboard—because engagement is everything.

The pandemic not only presented new challenges for teachers, but it also underscored the need for innovative approaches to get and keep students engaged in their learning journeys. Whether in-person or online, student engagement is vital for academic success and must be a top priority for educators. In my experience, one of the best ways to achieve this is by allowing students some control over learning.

For many teachers who love being at the center of their students' attention, stepping back from the front of the classroom may be difficult. However, student-centered learning is far more engaging and motivating for students. It should come as no surprise then, when students have a say in what and how they learn, they are more likely to retain the information being presented. By empowering students to take control of their own learning, teachers can help them develop crucial skills such as problem-solving, critical thinking, and self-direction. These are skills that will not only serve them well in school but will also be essential for when they leave school.

While it's certainly true that the transition towards student-centered learning can present a challenging paradigm shift for some educators, the role of administrative support in facilitating this shift is, without question, an invaluable one.

The Importance of Administrative Support

Mr. David Jenson, principal at Wise Middle School (Wise, Virginia), understood that some of his teachers might naturally revert to teacher-centered classrooms after returning to in-person learning following the pandemic. He knew that doing so could potentially hinder the progress his faculty made towards becoming a future-ready school prior to remote learning. Having observed his three school-aged children transform into self-directed, self-aware learners during the pandemic, Mr. Jenson was focused on maintaining the momentum his teachers built towards a more personalized learning environment. To that end, Mr. Jenson sent the following letter to his staff a few weeks before reopening school, not only welcoming them back, but urging them to remember the strides made during the pandemic.

Dear Colleagues,

As we approach the end of this unprecedented period, I would like to express my heartfelt gratitude to all of you for your unwavering commitment, dedication, and hard work during these trying times. The pandemic has posed significant challenges, and the way you have continued to show up for our students and their families is nothing short of remarkable.

I know that teaching during the pandemic has been incredibly challenging. You have had to adapt to new technologies, navigate uncertain schedules, and balance the demands of virtual and hybrid learning. Despite these challenges, you have continued to provide a high-quality education to our students, ensuring that they stay engaged and motivated throughout this difficult time. Your hard work and dedication have not gone unnoticed, and I am truly grateful for everything you have done.

I also want to acknowledge that many of us have lost loved ones during this pandemic. The grief and pain of losing someone close to us can be overwhelming, and I want you to know that we are here for you. As a school community, we will continue to support each other, lean on each other, and work together to move forward from this challenging time.

As we return to in-person learning, we have the opportunity to reconnect with our students and rebuild the strong relationships that are at the heart of our work. While we still face uncertainties and challenges, I know that together, we can overcome them. I am confident that we will emerge stronger and more resilient than ever before.

While the pandemic has brought many new challenges, it has also highlighted the need to engage students in sometimes new and innovative ways. Whether teaching in the physical classroom or the virtual one, we were reminded that student engagement is crucial for academic success and should be a top priority for all educators.

During the pandemic, my own children evolved into self-directed, self-aware learners. Jordan, my youngest, had the ability to sleep in a little later, had more flexibility and freedom during the day, and completed work at her own pace. As her father, I saw her develop a newfound love for learning that I have never seen before.

So, while it's understandable to want to return to past practices, I want to encourage you to remain focused on ensuring that students returning to school receive the same level of personalization they experienced while learning from home.

I am excited to see you all back in person and look forward to working with you as we navigate the challenges and opportunities ahead.

Best,
Mr. David Jenson
Principal, Wise Middle School

Looking back, while there were countless challenges, the pandemic also taught us valuable lessons about the importance of student engagement and the need for continued innovation in our teaching methods. By embracing the lessons learned during remote learning and incorporating more student-centered practices, we can ensure that our students remain engaged and motivated, no matter the subject area or learning modality.

As we continue to transition to a post-pandemic educational era, let's commit to proactively addressing the struggle for engagement. One way to do this is to leverage student-to-student feedback in our classrooms.

💡 EDI Strategy: Addressing the Struggle for Engagement with Student-to-Student Feedback

Fostering a culture in which all learning community members feel valued is essential. One of the best ways to achieve this is by providing students with clear directions and opportunities to deliver timely and meaningful feedback to their classmates. When giving feedback, students can often share their thoughts in a more relatable way with their peers than teachers. These interactions also tend to build rapport and trust among students.

Additionally, enabling students to provide feedback can help dismantle the hierarchy often present in traditional classrooms, where the teacher is seen as the sole expert. Instead, offering opportunities for students to give and receive feedback promotes a more collaborative learning environment where all class members feel their opinions and ideas are valued.

One of the most transformative experiences I've had as a teacher occurred when I began incorporating student-led feedback into my classroom. I always tried to provide my students with meaningful feedback on their work, but I was the only one doing that work. Once I allowed my students to provide feedback to one another, I saw our classroom culture become one in which students felt their voice finally mattered.

One student, Jamir, particularly benefited from this approach. Jamir was a gifted player on the basketball court but a shy and reserved student who struggled with confidence in the classroom. When I introduced peer feedback to the class, Jamir immediately came out of his shell. He began to speak up more in class, and his confidence soared as he saw that his peers respected and valued his insights. He went from being just a talented high school basketball player *in his own eyes* to someone who had much more to offer.

This experience demonstrated the power of breaking down the hierarchy that was present in my classroom. It also reminds me of the importance of providing students with opportunities to deliver timely and meaningful student-to-student feedback. By creating a more collaborative learning environment where class members felt their opinions and ideas were valued, I was finally able to maximize student agency and inclusivity for my students, something that I struggled with for a long time as a teacher.

One strategy that I find helpful to create opportunities for peer feedback is by using the 20-Minute Peer Feedback Activity. In this activity, students pair up and engage in a five-step process. Each step takes two minutes. After ten minutes, students switch roles. The following charts describe how to add the 20-Minute Peer Feedback Activity to any classroom.

Part 1	
0-2 minutes:	Partner A explains their process, product, or idea in two minutes. *For example, Partner A explains the theme and plot of their short story.*
2-4 minutes	Partner B asks clarifying questions without giving any feedback. *For example, Partner B asks clarifying questions about the characters and setting without giving any feedback.*

4-6 minutes	Partner B provides feedback to Partner A in the form of two things that worked well and one idea for improvement. *For example, Partner B provides feedback, praising Partner A's descriptive language and engaging dialogue but suggesting more development for a secondary character.*
6-8 minutes	Partner A paraphrases what they heard from Partner B, and both parties check for accuracy.
8-10 minutes	Partner A makes a list of future revisions.
Part 2	
10-12 minutes:	Partner B explains their process, product, or idea in two minutes.
12-14 minutes	Partner A asks clarifying questions without giving any feedback.
14-16 minutes	Partner A provides feedback to Partner A in the form of two things that worked well and one idea for improvement.
16-18 minutes	Partner B paraphrases what they heard from Partner B, and both parties check for accuracy.
18-20 minutes	Partner B makes a list of future revisions.

Besides creating a more collaborative learning environment, the 20-Minute Peer Feedback Activity can improve students' communication and listening skills. It can also enhance critical thinking skills by encouraging students to think about and reflect on their own work and the work of their classmates. It's also been my experience that by receiving feedback from their peers instead of their teacher, students can learn to accept constructive feedback in a positive manner and gain new perspectives and ideas that can enhance the creativity of their own work.

Engagement Starts with Us

As educators, our roles are central to the learning ecosystem. Our zeal, dedication, and fervor directly shape our students' engagement, accomplishments, and personal growth. By acknowledging the pivotal role our own engagement plays, we can create a learning environment that inspires and motivates our students.

This understanding stems from my experiences as a classroom teacher, instructional coach, and now a school administrator. I've observed firsthand that educators who exude a love for their work, exhibit confidence in their teaching capabilities, and demonstrate a profound understanding of teaching methodologies have an extraordinary influence on their students.

Research corroborates this observation, highlighting the profound impact of an engaged teacher on student outcomes. Many studies

> Educators who exude a love for their work, exhibit confidence in their teaching capabilities, and demonstrate a profound understanding of teaching methodologies have an extraordinary influence on their students.

(e.g., Sacier et al., 2020 and Cooper, 2014) establish a strong correlation between teacher engagement and student achievement, but it's the three dimensions of engagement (academic, intellectual, and social-emotional) mentioned in the previous section–that I believe are applicable to both students and adults.

Types of Teacher Engagement

Behavioral engagement refers to the participation and involvement of teachers and students in academic tasks and activities. For teachers, this might include lesson planning, classroom management, and collaboration with colleagues.

Cognitive engagement involves the investment of mental effort in understanding and mastering the subject matter. Engaged teachers continually seek to deepen their knowledge and hone their instructional strategies to better meet their students' needs.

Emotional engagement refers to the affective connections that teachers and students develop with the learning process, their peers, and the school community. Engaged teachers genuinely care about their students and work to create positive, supportive relationships with them.

So, to maximize student engagement, we must first focus on our own engagement as adults. The added stressors of the job certainly haven't made this easy, so if you find yourself hitting a wall with your practice or know someone else who is, here are some strategies I recommend to get recentered:

Reflect on Your Teaching Practice. Regular self-reflection allows teachers to assess their strengths and weaknesses, identify areas for improvement, and set professional goals. By continually evaluating our own teaching practices, we can develop the self-awareness necessary to improve our engagement and effectiveness in the classroom.

Seek Professional Development Opportunities. Engaged teachers are lifelong learners who constantly strive to expand their knowledge and skills. Actively participating in professional development opportunities, such as workshops, conferences, and online courses, can help teachers stay current with best practices, enhance their pedagogical skills, and maintain a high level of engagement.

Collaborate More with Colleagues. Collaboration with fellow teachers can provide valuable insights, support, and inspiration. Sharing ideas, discussing challenges, and working together on projects can not only improve our teaching practices but also foster a sense of community and engagement in our profession.

Lifelong learning is a hallmark of an engaged teacher. Actively participating in professional development opportunities such as workshops, conferences, and online courses helps keep pace with educational best practices, thereby enhancing pedagogical skills and maintaining a high degree of engagement.

Collaboration with colleagues can be invaluable. This exchange of ideas, experiences, and solutions can not only enrich our teaching practice but can also cultivate a sense of community within our schools.

One inspiring example of an educator who embodies high engagement levels is Mr. John Politano, a science teacher at Garnet Valley High School. His approach to nurturing student motivation is simple yet effective. He sets high expectations, creates relevance, and encourages active participation. His classes showcase a lively interaction and thoughtful lesson design, displaying his belief in designing an engaging and enriching learning environment.

Furthermore, Mr. Politano's ability to render learning relevant, authentic, and enjoyable is unmatched. By connecting the curriculum with real-world issues, incorporating students' interests and experiences, and providing opportunities for hands-on learning, he effectively sparks students' interest and builds student interactions into every activity.

He also provides a variety of instructional strategies, such as group work, debates, and simulations, to promote active learning. This has been instrumental in fostering student agency and participation in his classroom. His "a-ha" moment came several years ago when he sought feedback from his students on his teaching style. This simple reflective exercise altered his teaching approach, and changed the way he went about designing learning experiences for his students.

By showcasing Mr. Politano's exemplary work, I hope to inspire educators to adopt similar strategies, and, in turn, create a more engaging learning environment for their students. He believes in empowering students by providing opportunities to set personal learning goals, make informed choices about their learning activities, and reflect on their progress. This fosters the skills and habits essential for lifelong learning and future success.

I'm a firm believer that engagement starts with us, the adults. As educators, our level of engagement directly impacts our students' engagement and achievement. By focusing on our own professional growth, maintaining a healthy work-life balance, and implementing strategies to foster student engagement, we can create classrooms where all students are inspired, motivated, and empowered to learn.

EDI Strategy: Using Student-to-Teacher Feedback to Reflect on Our Practice

From my viewpoint, the feedback students provide teachers through end-of-unit surveys or end-of-year/semester course evaluations can be invaluable in helping teachers improve and refine their teaching. Soliciting student feedback has the additional benefit of allowing teachers to gather their students' input, and by doing so, give their students another chance to have their voices heard.

I've always been grateful for any opportunity to receive feedback from my students. One experience that stands out to me is when I was working as a communications instructor at the Williamson Trade College (Media, Pennsylvania). It was my first "real" teaching job, and I was nervous about what my students might say when completing end-of-course evaluations. At the same time, I was excited to hear their thoughts and gain a better perspective on my teaching.

Upon receiving my course evaluations, I was pleasantly surprised by the thoughtful comments from my students. Some of the most constructive feedback I've received included statements like, "I enjoyed the group projects because they helped me understand how the theories we learn apply in real life," and 'incorporating more real-world examples would help me understand the concepts better." This feedback provided me with actionable steps I then took to improve my teaching.

After reviewing my course evaluations, I was intrigued by the consistent mention of game-based activities from my students. To be more specific, one of the activities that received praise was the "Communication Relay," a game in which teams had to accurately relay a complex message to each other. This was intended to illustrate the concept of noise in communication. I had phased out this activity, assuming that the students were only focused on the fun element. However, the feedback revealed that students found it engaging and effective in understanding a complex concept in a fun and relatable way. Recognizing the value the students derived from this activity, I reintroduced it in the following semester, even expanding upon it by adding more layers of complexity and practical examples. The result was increased student engagement, participation, and a significant improvement in their understanding of communication noise.

This example reinforces the importance of soliciting student feedback and how valuable it can be in helping teachers improve and refine their teaching. It also calls attention to the importance of being open to hearing students' concerns and being willing to make appropriate changes to instruction when needed.

The interplay between student feedback and educator effectiveness is pivotal in evolving our educational practice. However, to truly tap into the potential of such feedback, it becomes crucial to recognize (and accept) that teaching is an iterative process, one that continually evolves and adapts based on reflection and inquiry.

As illustrated above, one concrete way to foster this culture of continuous improvement and reflection is through student surveys. Not only do they act as valuable feedback mechanisms for teachers, but they also serve to give students a voice in shaping their learning environments. Here are three tips I recommend to teachers interested in adding student-to-teacher surveys into their classroom routines:

Make surveys anonymous and don't grade them. Anonymity ensures that students can share their thoughts without fear of retribution or judgment. When students know their responses can't be traced back to them, they're likely to be more honest and thorough. Furthermore, not grading the feedback is crucial because it removes any incentive for students to provide insincere or "safe" responses to please the teacher or to secure a higher grade.

Make surveys simple and quick to complete. Time is a valuable resource in the educational setting for both teachers and students. Therefore, the feedback mechanism should be designed to respect this. A survey that is simple and quick to complete increases the likelihood of participation and can reduce the risk of survey fatigue that could lead to rushed or inaccurate responses. It also means that students can concentrate their effort on providing meaningful insights.

Be sure your survey questions ask what you want to find out. The most effective feedback is targeted and specific. The questions included in the survey should be carefully curated to provide insights on pedagogy, instruction, curriculum, workload, pace, environment, relationships, or any other aspect you're interested in improving. The survey should be seen as a tool for eliciting specific, actionable feedback that can lead to beneficial changes in the classroom.

Embracing student-to-teacher feedback does more than merely refine our teaching practices. It is a powerful tool for empowering students, giving them a sense of ownership over their learning, and encouraging their active participation in the educational process. It fosters a democratic and collaborative culture where students feel their voices matter. This not only cultivates a more engaging and respectful classroom environment but also nurtures essential life skills in our students. As we continue to navigate the evolving landscape of education, let's empower our students, respect their insights, and open doors to more inclusive and engaging learning experiences.

Teacher Talk vs. Student Talk

In my 25+ years in education, I've been on a quest to identify strategies that can not only spark student interest, but also sustain their engagement and deepen their understanding. One such strategy is to create an environment in which students can connect, ask questions, and share openly. Yet, research reveals that in many classrooms, teachers tend to talk between 70-80% of the class time on average, with this percentage increasing as students' progress through higher grade levels.

Dr. Janet Clinton, Director of the Teacher and Teaching Effectiveness Research Hub at the University of Melbourne, Australia, discovered that on average, teachers ask a staggering two hundred questions per day. This prompted me to wonder, how many questions do students ask per day? Astoundingly, Dr. Clinton's research indicates that students only ask two questions per week on average—not per day, but per week! Dr. Clinton calls this Teacher Talk vs. Student Talk.

Teacher talk refers to the time a teacher spends talking during a lesson, while student talk refers to the amount of time students spend participating in discussions and contributing their ideas. Her research has shown that when teachers dominate the conversation and do most of the talking, students are less likely to be engaged and may struggle to retain information. On the other hand, when students are given the opportunity to participate in discussions and share their own ideas, they are more likely to be engaged and motivated to learn.

As educators, it is natural for us to want to share our knowledge and expertise with our students. However, Dr. Clinton's findings demonstrate that there needs to be a delicate balance between teacher talk and student talk in the classroom. In the end, learning is more effective when students have the opportunity to engage in discussions and contribute their own ideas.

So, let us embark on a transformative journey as educators, shifting the balance from teacher talk to student talk, empowering our students to take charge of their own learning experiences, and ultimately, helping them unlock their full potential as learners.

In my career, I've been able to work with many outstanding educators across the country. What I have learned is that when teachers turn the learning over to their students, many positive outcomes begin to surface. Some examples of these outcomes include:

> In my own district (Garnet Valley) when students actively participate in their own learning, they are more likely to retain information and achieve academic success. This was true whether the learning occurs in a physical classroom or in our virtual classrooms.

> In the Interboro School District (Prospect Park, Pennsylvania), when students have the opportunity to contribute their ideas and take an active role in their learning, they are more likely to be motivated and invested in the process.

> In the Kingsway Regional School District (Woolwich Township, New Jersey), student-centered learning fosters critical thinking skills. By encouraging students to ask questions, share their own ideas, and engage in discussions, teachers in Kingsway help students develop critical thinking skills and learn to think for themselves.

> In the Centennial School District (Warminster, Pennsylvania), student-centered learning promotes equity. By allowing students to participate in discussions and contribute their ideas, educators in Centennial help ensure that all voices are heard and that all students feel valued and included.

By fostering a classroom atmosphere in which students can connect, ask questions, and share openly, we empower students to take control of their learning, increase engagement, and unlock their full potential.

EDI Strategy: Leveraging Class Discussions to Get Students Talking

Class discussions are a powerful tool for fostering student engagement, motivation, and collaboration. When executed effectively, they can lead to improved communication skills, increased student involvement, and even higher grades. However, class discussions can also be misused, resulting in unequal participation and low student engagement levels.

In my work with teachers in Garnet Valley and elsewhere, I have found success in building student interactions by implementing the discussion guidelines below. While there are many examples available online, the guidelines below, adapted from Columbia University's Center for Teaching and Learning, have proven effective in my experience. These strategies are organized into three key areas: planning, engaging, and wrapping up classroom discussions.

Planning for Classroom Discussions: Successful class discussions require careful planning and preparation. When planning for class discussions consider the following steps:

- Determine the content and skills you want students to learn and apply during the discussion. Communicate the purpose of the discussion to help students understand its relevance to their learning.
- Clearly outline the expected quality and quantity of student contributions and provide examples of substantive responses. Offer guidance on how students can contribute to their peers' live responses or online posts.

Engaging in Classroom Discussions: With the planning and preparation complete, consider these essential aspects during the discussion:

- Clarify how the teacher will facilitate the discussion and participate in asynchronous discussions. Establish student expectations for engagement, such as response requirements, group work, and participation guidelines.
- Involving students in class discussions allows more voices and viewpoints to be heard. Providing time for students to think before, during, and after the discussion encourages more meaningful contributions and creates opportunities for a wider range of students to participate.

Wrapping Up Classroom Discussions: An effective wrap-up is crucial for ensuring discussions align with learning objectives and reinforce student understanding. Consider the following:

- Allow students to reflect on and share what they have learned, helping them make connections between the discussion and other course materials. This process also enables the teacher to assess the discussion's effectiveness and make adjustments for future sessions.
- Use the wrap-up as an opportunity to gauge how the discussion went and identify areas for clarification or improvement. This ongoing assessment helps refine and enhance future discussions for greater student success.

Crafting engaging class discussions is an essential skill for teachers in any learning environment. By focusing on planning, engaging, and wrapping up discussions, we can create interactive, inclusive, and meaningful learning experiences.

Yes, You are an Asynchronous Teacher

In today's digital age, every teacher is an asynchronous teacher, whether consciously acknowledged or not. Asynchronous learning (learning that occurs outside the constraints of time and place) has become an intrinsic part of our educational framework. When the bell rings to dismiss students, be it to change classes or at the end of the day, learning is expected to continue.

Teachers play a pivotal role in shaping this continued learning experience as students navigate tasks and assignments beyond the physical classroom. However, there's a common misconception, especially in post-pandemic times, that asynchronous learning is primarily for virtual classrooms. This misconception overlooks the potential of asynchronous learning in fostering interaction and collaboration among students, regardless of the learning format.

For instance, my involvement in creating the eSchool@Garnet-Valley program revealed the effectiveness of asynchronous activities. These activities, especially those that incorporated reflection moments, allowed students to engage with the content at their own pace without the immediate pressure to respond. It was enlightening to observe how this approach led students to a deeper understanding of the content and a heightened self-awareness of their learning process.

To further illustrate this point, let's consider a chart I came across while collaborating with the Global Online Academy (GOA). This chart provides a concise comparison of synchronous and asynchronous learning strategies, explaining the "when," "why," and "how" of employing these strategies in the modern classroom. The chart, while initially developed for teachers new to online learning, offers valuable insights for teachers across various formats:

	Synchronous Learning	Asynchronous Learning
When?	✔ Reflecting on less complex issues. ✔ Getting acquainted. ✔ Assigning tasks.	✔ Reflecting on complex issues. ✔ When synchronous meetings cannot be scheduled.
Why?	✔ Students become more committed and motivated because a quick response is expected.	✔ Students have more time to reflect because the teacher does not expect an immediate answer.
How?	✔ When students are not in the classroom, teachers can use video conferencing apps or software to connect with students or parents.	✔ Use asynchronous tools such as email, discussion groups, collaborative docs, Padlet, and other tech tools to provide asynchronous learning opportunities.

One of the crucial advantages of asynchronous learning is that it's an effective way to differentiate instruction. In my visits to various classrooms, I've seen students who often finish tasks early. Traditionally, such students are either given more work (e.g., more math problems or more questions to answer) or told to "work ahead." However, this approach could inadvertently penalize students who are simply working at their own pace. This situation necessitates an informed discussion on two educational approaches that are often debated: enrichment and acceleration.

Enrichment vs. Acceleration

The long-standing debate concerning the choice between enrichment activities (allowing students to delve deeper into specific concepts) and acceleration (letting students move swiftly through parts of the curriculum they easily grasp) has been part of numerous faculty meetings over the years. The most pragmatic response to this debate is that both strategies can be effective when applied appropriately. Enrichment can expand and diversify students' educational experiences, and research supports that students accelerating through parts of the curriculum also see enhanced academic achievement.

To illustrate the effective implementation of these strategies within the context of asynchronous learning, let's explore an alternative example from Ms. Johnson, a 7th-grade math teacher at Lakeview Middle School in San Francisco, California. Ms. Johnson faced a common predicament many educators encounter: meeting the needs of students who regularly finish early or master content beyond their grade level. This includes students with Gifted Individualized Education Plans (GIEPs). Her solution was a balanced blend of enrichment and acceleration activities that leveraged asynchronous learning.

Ms. Johnson decided to employ enrichment activities for her students with GIEPs, aiming to enhance their collaborative skills, listening abilities, and social awareness. Drawing on her years of teaching experience, Ms. Johnson discovered that incorporating asynchronous learning activities into her lessons was instrumental in differentiating her instruction.

To meet the needs of her GIEP students, Ms. Johnson designed various asynchronous enrichment activities allowing students to dive deeper into the mathematical concepts covered in class. These activities were self-paced, providing students the freedom to work according to their own timeline and challenge themselves accordingly.

For instance, when teaching about algebraic expressions, Ms. Johnson designed optional problem sets for her students to tackle. These problem sets required students to apply learned concepts in novel ways which promoted a deeper understanding of the concept. To encourage collaboration and social awareness, students with GIEPs were grouped and tasked with presenting their problem-solving methods to the class.

Besides problem sets, Ms. Johnson also integrated asynchronous discussion forums for the class. These forums enabled students to engage in more in-depth discussions about the mathematical concepts, sharing their insights, and posing questions to their peers. This asynchronous collaboration amplified students' comprehension of the subject matter while also bolstering their communication and critical thinking skills.

In Ms. Johnson's words, "the asynchronous learning activities have been the most effective way to challenge my gifted students and deepen their understanding of class topics."

These activities enable students to work independently, collaborate, apply their creativity, and hone their critical thinking skills. By incorporating asynchronous learning opportunities into her curriculum, Ms. Johnson was able to optimize student agency, inclusivity, and fully embody the EDI framework to build interactions and design learning experiences that cater to her students' unique needs. One way to do this that works with any grade level and content area is by adding asynchronous, reflective journaling activities.

EDI Strategy: Using Reflective Journaling as an Asynchronous Activity

In the ever-evolving world of education, it's important for teachers to continuously seek new ways to engage students and create more inclusive, diverse, and flexible learning environments. As discussed in an earlier section and worth repeating, traditional classroom delivery can sometimes be challenging for some students and it's not always the best setting for the exposition of rich or difficult material. Providing asynchronous learning opportunities can ensure all student voices are heard and make student learning more visible.

One strategy that I find fits nicely as an asynchronous activity is reflective journaling. Reflective journaling offers students an opportunity to engage in self-directed learning outside the traditional classroom setting. It encourages students to analyze their own learning and identify areas for improvement. I find this sense of ownership motivates students to engage more actively, leading to better connections in the in-person settings.

Mrs. Thompson, an 11th grade English teacher in Virginia, introduces reflective journaling to her students early in the school year. She finds this practice gives students the space to express their thoughts and feelings without the constraints of classroom dynamics. She also finds it an essential way to *Effectively Design Instruction* for introspective learners who thrive in self-directed learning environments.

Here are six prompts that Mrs. Thompson uses to inspire her students to think critically and reflect on their learning experiences. These prompts are designed to encourage students to think deeply about their learning experiences, personal growth, and the connections between their education and the world around them. While these examples come from a high school classroom, I believe they can also be adapted to any grade level:

1. Describe a moment in class this week that challenged you. What made it difficult, and how did you overcome the challenge? What did you learn from the experience?
2. Think about a recent lesson or topic you found particularly interesting. Explain why it captured your attention and how it connects to your personal interests or experiences.

3. Choose one skill or concept you've learned recently that you believe will be valuable in your future. Explain why you think it's important and how you plan to apply it in real-life situations.

4. Describe a memorable moment from class or a school activity that made you proud or happy. What made the experience special, and how did it impact your perspective on learning or personal growth?

5. Reflect on the role of creativity in your learning process. How do you express your creativity in different subjects or assignments, and how does it contribute to your understanding of the material?

6. Consider a time when you made a mistake or encountered a setback in your learning. How did you feel at the time, and how did you handle the situation? What lessons did you learn from the experience, and how have you applied them since?

Reflective journaling is a powerful tool for creating asynchronous learning opportunities that empower students to take control of their educational journey. Give this strategy a try the next time you want to provide your students with self-directed learning outside the traditional classroom setting.

Connection Before Content

Fostering healthy connections with students not only develops a sense of belonging but also catalyzes heightened engagement and more profound learning. As educators, our focus must extend beyond purely delivering content. We need to construct an environment where students feel genuinely connected and supported.

Recent findings from a study conducted by Youth Truth reveal a disheartening reality—numerous students feel disengaged from their education due to home distractions and a lack of meaningful tasks. Surprisingly, only half of the students surveyed felt that they had positive relationships with their teachers. These revelations underscore the necessity for cultivating connections in the classroom, a factor that research has shown significantly augments the overall student learning experience.

In my journey as an educator, three strategies have proven instrumental in building these crucial relationships with students:

Connect with Students One-on-One. Spending time to connect with each student individually has proven immensely fruitful. Scheduling one-on-one meetings to understand students' personal circumstances, aspirations, and ideas helps build a deeper, more personal connection.

Prioritize Relationships and Conversations. Develop opportunities for substantive connections and conversations within the classroom, regardless of whether the learning environment is in-person, remote, or hybrid. Stimulate thought-provoking discussions and endorse students sharing their unique perspectives. This strategy fosters a sense of belonging and encourages students to actively engage in class dialogues.

Relevance Over Routine. Assignments should offer more than just an obligation to be fulfilled. Incorporate projects that demand multidisciplinary learning and development of real-world skills, thus boosting their relevance for students.

By emphasizing connections before content, we will be able to cultivate an inclusive, engaging learning space that supports student autonomy and maximizes the potential of every learner.

EDI Strategy: From Feedback to Feedforward When Providing Teacher-to-Student Feedback

A profound realization in my teaching career was understanding the true purpose of providing feedback. During a department meeting, my head of department, while reviewing a student's assignment, pointed out that my notes, albeit accurate, came across as overly critical. He subtly reminded me, "The goal of feedback is to enhance a student's performance, not to demoralize them."

This was a significant turning point for me, highlighting that feedback should ideally be a positive learning experience for students. From then on, I adopted the concept of "Feedforward"—a method that emphasizes future potential rather than past mistakes.

Feedforward is characterized by offering constructive suggestions focused on future actions. It equips students with actionable insights to improve their forthcoming performances, encouraging them to shape their future outcomes positively.

The practical application of Feedforward in classrooms and beyond can be facilitated through six effective strategies:

Six Strategies to Feedforward

Encourage Self-Reflection
Prompt individuals to reflect on their own performance and identify areas for improvement.

Follow Up and Support
Offer ongoing support and follow-up after providing feedforward. Check in on progress, provide additional resources or guidance if needed, and celebrate achievements and milestones along the way.

Supportive and Encouraging Tone
Feedforward should be delivered in a supportive and constructive manner, focusing on strengths and potential growth areas.
It should motivate students to embrace change and strive for continuous improvement.

Focus on Growth Mindset
Encourage students to embrace challenges, view mistakes as learning experiences, and persist in their efforts to improve.

Proactive Nature
Feedforward is given prior to the completion of a task or activity, allowing students to consider and integrate the suggestions or guidance into their performance.

Actionable and Specific Suggestions
Feedforward should be specific, clear, and related to the task or activity at hand, enabling students to understand what steps to take for enhanced performance.

Our students' experiences, be they positive or negative, depend significantly on our feedforward. By incorporating this approach, we empower students to take charge of their learning journey and foster a growth mindset, allowing them to view challenges as stepping stones towards development. The result is a learning environment that encourages growth, resilience, and positivity, inspiring students to strive for their highest potential.

Embracing the Fun Theory

In 2001, Stockholm, Sweden, became the site of an ingenious experiment that challenged conventional thinking and made seemingly ordinary activities extraordinary. The creative minds at Volkswagen, spearheading what they called "The Fun Theory," transformed a flight of stairs at a subway station into a larger-than-life piano, each step playing a unique note as pedestrians ascended or descended. This whimsical intervention resulted in a whopping 66% increase in stair use over the adjacent escalator. The lesson? Fun can powerfully influence behavior.

This captivating tale has significant implications for education, shedding light on how we can invigorate our instructional design and foster student agency and inclusivity. By weaving elements of fun and experiential learning into our pedagogy, we can create classroom environments that inspire active participation and deepen student engagement.

> By weaving elements of fun and experiential learning into our pedagogy, we can create classroom environments that inspire active participation and deepen student engagement.

Mrs. Jacqueline Li, an elementary school teacher in Los Angeles, California, exemplifies this approach. After learning about the Volkswagen experiment, Mrs. Li infused her teaching philosophy with the essence of "The Fun Theory," transforming her classroom into a hub of curiosity, joy, and learner autonomy.

Mrs. Li started by redesigning her physical classroom. The once-drab space bloomed with color, inspiring lighting, and displays that sparked creativity. Educational materials related to current units of study shared wall space with student artwork and posters of notable community members.

Next, Mrs. Li introduced self-paced, interactive learning stations. Each station focused on a different element of the curriculum, incorporating hands-on activities, multimedia resources, and group discussions. This shift in teaching strategy not only increased accessibility for diverse learners but also fostered student ownership of learning paths.

Embracing the gamification aspect of "The Fun Theory," Mrs. Li introduced gaming elements into her teaching. Students designed avatars for their online profiles, received badges for demonstrating focus or resilience, and embarked on learning quests and challenges that aligned with the curriculum.

Drawing from cognitive psychology, the essence of "The Fun Theory" lies in its potential to activate students' intrinsic motivation, leading to a more profound and enjoyable learning experience. However, implementing this theory isn't without challenges. It requires creativity, time, and resources, and it may not suit every learning style or content area. Yet, I believe its transformative power in fostering engagement and inclusivity makes it worth exploring.

More than a single method or tool, "The Fun Theory" symbolizes a mindset that sees learning as a joyful, immersive, and memorable journey. Just as the piano stairs in Stockholm altered pedestrians' behaviors one step at a time, a classroom infused with "The Fun Theory" can influence students' educational journey, prompting them to engage with their learning actively.

As educators, our mission extends beyond delivering content—it's about designing learning experiences that spark curiosity, foster interdependence, and empower students. By integrating principles of the "Fun Theory" into our classrooms, we can cultivate an engaging learning environment where each student's potential is recognized and nurtured. The transformative power of a well-designed learning environment can indeed change a student's educational path, making each step an exciting note in their symphony of learning.

💡 EDI Strategy: Creating Collaborative Learning Opportunities that Foster Interdependence

Collaborative learning is a powerful teaching strategy that can lead to deeper understanding and higher levels of engagement among students. In Garnet Valley, our Instructional Design Coaches support teachers to create dynamic learning environments that foster collaboration and encourage immersive and memorable learning experiences. By offering opportunities for students to work together and learn from one another, teachers can help break down barriers and build bridges across diverse backgrounds and perspectives.

One effective way to bring a class together is by placing students in challenging situations that require teamwork. If an assignment is relatively simple, students may find it easier to complete it individually, with minimal interaction and exchange of ideas. On the other hand, a complex task that is challenging, engaging, and multilayered naturally lends itself to collaboration, as it becomes arduous to accomplish alone.

Complex activities are not merely challenging; they stimulate intellectual curiosity, encourage creative problem-solving, and involve several intertwined layers that require unraveling. Such activities necessitate what David Johnson calls "positive interdependence," in his book, *Cooperating in the Classroom* (2008). This is a state where the attainment of a goal, successful task completion, and achieving a commendable grade are closely tied to the collective effort and shared knowledge of the team.

An effective approach to fostering such collaboration is through the introduction of rigorous projects that push students to engage with real-world problems. A prime example of this is the student escape room, a popular activity gaining traction among educators. Recently, Mrs. Meredith McNaulty, a third-grade teacher at Garnet Valley Elementary School (Glen Mills, PA) used an escape room to teach her students about fractions. Like many classrooms, fractions were not a popular topic among these third graders. Nevertheless, as an important part of the curriculum that often causes anxiety among students and their parents, this teacher sought a novel approach to introducing the subject.

Having employed games like BreakoutEDU for other content, Meredith felt confident that, at the very least, the students would have fun—even if the learning wasn't optimal. Students were divided into small groups and given a set of clues to solve in order to "escape" the room. As the class collaborated to decipher the clues, students utilized higher-level thinking, communication, and problem-solving skills.

The advantages of this activity were evident. Students were more engaged and invested in their learning, and working with peers from different backgrounds and learning styles promoted greater inclusivity in the classroom. While the benefits mentioned were significant, the true value emerged at the end of the class when students shared their learnings. Never before had a third-grade classroom been so enthusiastic about discussing fractions. Additionally, since the clues were designed to connect with items in the classroom, students found visualizing the concept easier than ever before.

The essence of collaborative learning, as demonstrated through activities like student escape rooms, resonates strongly with the principles outlined in "The Fun Theory." By infusing learning with elements of fun, challenge, and engagement, we can create a vibrant classroom environment where students are not merely absorbing information but actively participating in their education.

The excitement of unraveling clues in an escape room or working together to solve a complex problem transforms learning from a solitary task into a shared adventure. This alignment with "The Fun Theory" not only enhances understanding but also fosters a sense of community and interdependence among students.

Many educators might feel hesitant to implement collaborative learning activities due to the concern over "freeriding," where a select few students shoulder the entire workload. Based on my experience, there are several proactive measures teachers can take to mitigate the risk of freeriding during group activities. These include:

Establish Smaller Teams: Form smaller teams of four or five students at most. Smaller groups foster greater visibility, making nonparticipation less likely.

Promote Individual Accountability. Ensure students are accountable individually as well as collectively. One way to do this could be to administer a short quiz at the end of the session, testing individual understanding of the learning objectives from the collaborative activity.

Assign Purposeful Roles. Craft team roles that are both meaningful and relevant to the task at hand. Avoid episodic roles like timekeeping, which lack intellectual engagement and may inadvertently encourage freeriding. Instead, allocate roles such as project manager, quality monitor, or leader for each subtask. These roles can instill a sense of ownership in students and allow for performance evaluation based on successful role fulfillment.

Encourage Self and Peer Evaluation. Have students assess their own and their teammates' participation and effort. This encourages reflection on individual contributions and holds each student accountable for their part in the project. Triangulating these self-assessments with your evaluations as a teacher can provide a holistic view of each student's performance.

By employing innovative activities such as student escape rooms, teachers can *Effectively Design Instruction* and craft experiences that truly engage and challenge their students. This is just one example of how collaborative learning can transform the classroom experience. With the right tools and strategies, you can cultivate a new generation of learners who are motivated, empowered, and prepared to face the challenges of the "next normal."

Reflecting on Building Interactions

The Building Interactions theme explored the key strategies for getting and keeping students engaged in their learning. These strategies included: student-to-student feedback, teacher-to-student feedback, student-to-teacher feedback, asynchronous learning, synchronous learning, and collaborative learning.

By encouraging students to give and receive feedback from their peers, we can promote active learning among our students and create a more collaborative learning environment. Teachers play a critical role in providing feedback that is constructive, supportive, and tailored to each student's needs. Similarly, when students provide feedback to their teachers, it can help them to identify areas for improvement and make adjustments to their instructional approach.

By leveraging the EDI strategies provided in this theme and others, my hope is that you add them to your teacher toolkit, so that you can create a learning environment that truly maximizes the potential of every student in your classroom. As you reflect on the information presented in this chapter, consider the following questions:

1. How can you ensure that your students actively participate in the learning process and avoid reverting back to a teacher-centered classroom that Mr. Jenson warned his faculty against?

2. What steps can you take, similar to those in Mr. Politano's Science classes, to make learning more relevant and authentic for your students?

3. How can you apply the research of Dr. Clinton and empower your students to ask more questions in class?

4. What steps can you take to ensure you are designing instruction that caters to the diverse needs of your students, including those with GIEPs, as demonstrated by Mr. Stevenson's example?

5. In what ways can you establish healthy connections with students that not only fosters a sense of belonging, but gets student activity participating in your classroom?

6. How can you bring "The Fun Theory" to life in your classroom, and–similar to Mrs. Li and Mrs. McNaulty–create an inclusive and engaging learning environment for every student in your classroom?

By reflecting on these questions and revisiting the examples and strategies provided in this chapter, you'll be better equipped to build even better student interactions in your classroom.

~

CHAPTER III

EDI Theme: Presenting Content

"Technology will not replace great teachers but technology in the hands of great teachers can be transformational."

–George Couros, educator and author

Our third theme stands at the intersection of knowledge and experience, technology and pedagogy, innovation and tradition. Here, we dive headfirst into one of the most crucial aspects of teaching in our increasingly digital age: Presenting Content. Our journey will take us through the exploration of effective strategies and innovative techniques that will transform the way you approach lesson design, LMS organization, and content delivery.

Before diving into the in-depth exploration of this essential subject, allow me to outline the journey we'll be taking together in this chapter:

EDI Focus	Benefits to Students	Try It Out
Setting Up Consistent Course Navigation.	Consistent course organization ensures easy access to learning materials, creates a predictable pattern, and helps students navigate the digital course.	*Edvative Learning* LMS Rubric (p. 101)
Using the Physical Room Layout to Create Connections.	Classroom set up aids in creating a welcoming and familiar learning environment and can help students to form emotional connections to their learning.	Six options for classroom seating arrangements (p. 109)
Digital Page Layout–Simple, but Not Simplistic.	A clear, concise digital layout reduces cognitive load and allows students to focus on understanding the subject matter rather than being overwhelmed by unnecessary complexity.	Three areas of focus for effective page layout (p. 112)
Nurturing Parental Engagement in today's technology-rich classrooms.	Active parental engagement fosters a supportive learning environment both at school and at home.	Parent Empathy Mapping (p. 116)

EDI Focus	Benefits to Students	Try It Out
Be a curator, not a dumper, when it comes to adding resources to an LMS.	When educators carefully select and present relevant content it prevents information overload, increases engagement, and supports meaningful understanding of the curriculum.	Listen to the Cult of Pedagogy podcast (p. 122)
Crafting personalized instructional videos for your students.	Custom videos created by teachers can enhance students' comprehension, because they are already familiar with their teacher's style, voice, and mannerisms.	Five tips for creating effective videos (p. 125)

We are all too familiar with the proverb, "Content is King," but in an age where the average attention span is constantly shrinking and the battle for students' focus intensifies, the manner in which we present content is becoming equally regal. The key lies in the artful balance of making your lessons engaging, inclusive, and effective. This chapter focuses on just that, offering you a compass to navigate this exciting terrain.

Over the course of this chapter, we will uncover six EDI Strategies for Presenting Content, each one offering a unique lens to view and approach your lesson design. From the captivating power of storytelling–drawing students into a world where learning becomes an adventure–to the judicious use of diverse media formats–videos, podcasts, interactive games–each strategy unravels a new layer in engaging students with differing learning styles and preferences.

Our journey doesn't stop there. We'll explore the benefits of culturally responsive teaching and explore how integrating real-world examples and problem-solving tasks can turn abstract concepts into tangible skills. This chapter will also highlight the ways in which everyday technologies can be woven into your lessons to create a dynamic and authentic learning experience for students.

So, whether you're a novice educator navigating your first LMS or a seasoned teacher looking to infuse more creativity and innovation into your lessons, this chapter will arm you with insights and strategies to elevate your presentation skills. As you turn these pages, anticipate a journey of discovery and growth, where each section unfolds a new path towards more engaging, inclusive, and effective content presentation. Are you ready to transform your teaching practice and make every lesson a memorable learning experience for your students? Let's begin this journey together.

Design is Not Decoration

In the world of art, there is a saying that "form follows function." This principle, coined by architect Louis Sullivan, suggests that the design of an object should be primarily based upon its intended function or purpose. Similarly, in the world of education, the goal of instructional design is to create accessible and inclusive learning environments that promote student agency and inclusivity. Although often misunderstood, instructional design is not merely decorating resources in the LMS.

To illustrate this concept, let's consider the story of Longwood Gardens, the one-thousand-acre botanic garden located in Kennett Square, Pennsylvania. Since 1921, Longwood Gardens has been one of the premier horticultural display gardens in the United States and is open to visitors year-round to enjoy native and exotic plants and horticulture, events and performances, seasonal and themed attractions, as well as educational lectures, courses, and workshops.

While the garden has always been visually stunning, when first opened to the public the design was not inclusive or accessible to everyone that wanted to visit. The pathways were too narrow for those using wheelchairs, there were no tactile elements for individuals with visual impairments, and despite the multicultural area, the signage was not available in multiple languages for non-English speakers. In an effort to make the gardens the most visually appealing horticultural display in the country, the landscape designers failed to consider the diversity of visitors who would be touring the grounds.

Recognizing these shortcomings, Pierre du Pont, Longwood Gardens' trustee, consulted with disability advocates, non-English speaking residents, and experts in inclusive design to make his prized garden more accessible for everyone. Within a year, Longwood Gardens widened the pathways, added tactile elements, and created multilingual signage. By re-evaluating the Gardens' priorities and focusing on accessibility and inclusion, du Pont transformed his masterpiece into a space that was not only breathtaking but also welcoming and enjoyable for the entire community. Anyone who visits Longwood Gardens today can appreciate these thoughtful adjustments.

For those reading this book not familiar with Longwood, the Gardens provide a wide range of continuing education opportunities for both novice and experienced gardeners. Their programs cover ornamental horticulture, landscape design, visual arts, and floral design. They also offer K-12 programs tied to Next Generation Science Standards, with a focus on environmental stewardship, biodiversity, and plant propagation.

College and university students can participate in internships across 16 specializations, including arboriculture, conservatory management, and turf management. International students can also participate in internships in education, library science, marketing and public relations, and ornamental horticulture.

For those interested in pursuing a career in horticulture, Longwood offers a two-year, tuition-free Professional Gardener program. They also partner with the University of Delaware to offer the Longwood Graduate Program in Public Horticulture for those seeking leadership positions in botanical gardens and other horticultural institutions.

Much like du Pont's approach to redesigning Longwood Gardens, educators must prioritize *intentional* instructional design to create accessible and inclusive learning environments for our students. While color, font style, and page layout can increase engagement, the true essence of instructional design goes beyond mere aesthetics in the LMS.

By acknowledging and addressing the diverse needs, abilities, and experiences of our students, we can *Effectively Design Instruction* and heighten engagement and create inclusive learning environments that benefit everyone. In doing so, we can empower our students to flourish and succeed, just like the vibrant plants and flowers at Longwood Gardens.

💡 EDI Strategy: Setting Up Consistent Course Navigation

A well-structured Learning Management System (LMS) forms the backbone of today's modern educational landscape. Both learners and their supporting network, including parents and support teachers, benefit immensely from clear and easy access to course materials, assignments, and resources. A strategically organized LMS minimizes time spent searching for information and maximizes the actual learning experience.

One key aspect of organizing an LMS is using a consistent folder structure and common nomenclature within and across all courses and subjects. This involves organizing materials in a logical and intuitive way and using consistent naming conventions for folders and files. For example, you might have a main folder for each course, with subfolders for different units or topics within the course. Within each unit folder, you could have separate folders for readings, assignments, videos, and other resources. There are several benefits to using a consistent folder structure and common nomenclature in your LMS, including:

Improved Navigation and Accessibility. When students and parents can easily find and access materials, it saves time and helps to minimize confusion and frustration. Consistent folder structure and naming conventions help to make it clear where to find specific resources and how they are organized.

Enhanced Collaboration. Consistent folder structures and naming conventions can foster better collaboration among educators. When multiple teachers, particularly those supporting students with special needs, use the same LMS, consistency ensures everyone works in harmony. It also reduces time spent on navigating through different courses.

Improved Efficiency and Productivity. Using a consistent folder structure and common nomenclature can save teachers time and effort that would otherwise be spent searching for and organizing materials.

While there is no universally agreed-upon format, using a consistent folder structure and common nomenclature is an essential aspect of organizing and managing course materials in today's schools. By implementing and adhering to a consistent structure, teachers can improve navigation, collaboration, and productivity, and ultimately, create a better learning experience for their students and those who support them.

One crucial, yet often underemphasized benefit of a well-structured LMS, is its instrumental role in personalized learning. By creating an intuitive and consistent navigation system, teachers can better analyze student activity and engagement. This organization does not only facilitate easier access to content, but also cultivates a data-rich environment that can help inform personalized instruction.

With every click, download, and online interaction, students leave a digital footprint. This data, when properly analyzed, reveals patterns and trends in student engagement and performance. For example, teachers might notice a correlation between the time spent on specific course materials and success in subsequent assessments, or identify frequently accessed resources, indicating areas of higher interest or possibly greater difficulty.

Additionally, an organized LMS can support differentiated instruction by allowing teachers to tailor resources to meet individual learning styles and needs. For instance, within a unit folder, teachers could include various resource types, like readings, interactive activities, and video lectures catered to different learning modalities. This variety not only provides students with a choice in their learning pathway, but also empowers them to take ownership of their education.

My dissertation research revealed a profound effect the lack of consistent folder structures had on special education teachers. For instance, one participant noted, "when regular education teachers do not follow a consistent LMS structure, special education teachers are left to navigate the many courses they are assigned to support blindly." Due to LMS inconsistencies, special education teachers reported spending most of their time "tracking down assignments" in the LMS instead of using that time to support students. If we are to truly *Effectively Design Instruction*, schools will need to adopt a consistent folder structure for their teachers to follow. If your school has not provided an LMS rubric or checklist, take a look at the QM Course Design Standards for K-12 found on the *Quality Matters* website or use the following LMS Rubric adapted by our team at *Edvative Learning*.

Course Structure & Communication	Present	Not Present
The course syllabus is easily accessible.		
Course policies (netiquette, communication practices, expectations, email response time, late assignments, proper writing techniques, self-introduction, etc.) are clearly defined and outlined.		
Course learning objectives/goals are outlined.		
Course grading policies are clearly stated. Example: teachers should provide clear instructions to students on how to submit work online, provide rubrics on how the paper will be graded, and return the paper with comments to the student in a timely manner.		
Course instructions articulate or link to tutorials and resources that answer basic questions related to research, writing, technology, etc.		
Technical help information is provided for students.		

Engagement & Learning Objectives	Present	Not Present
Course provides activities and assignments that foster student interaction.		
Course offers students some control over time, place, path, and/or pace.		
Learning activities foster instructor-student, content-student, and, if appropriate to this course, student-student interaction.		
Learning activities foster instructor-student, content-student, and, if appropriate to this course, student-student interaction. The learning objectives of the course are clearly stated and understandable to the student.		
The learning objectives of the course are articulated and specified on the module/unit level.		
Accessibility & Usability	**Present**	**Not Present**
Course uses multiple communication tools to address learners and varying learning styles (announcements, email, videos, discussion boards).		
Course provides guides, prompts, checklists, and templates as needed.		
Course demonstrates sensitivity to readability issues.		

Accessibility & Usability	Present	Not Present
Use naming conventions and digital tools to allow for easy navigation.		
Course uses clear and consistent nomenclature and folder structure.		

Designing for Contribution, Not Consumption

Picture a classroom where students are not just passive listeners, but active participants in their learning journey. They engage in vibrant discussions, pose thought-provoking questions, share unique insights, and bridge new content with their existing knowledge base. As educators, this dynamic learning environment is what we strive to create. Throughout previous chapters, we have examined the pivotal components of student engagement and the crafting of meaningful educational experiences. The key to transforming your classroom into an active learning hub, however, lies in skillfully integrating these elements into your content delivery.

As a career educator, I have seen the significance of achieving a balance between delivering quality content and designing educational experiences that allow students to steer their own learning. In this section, I want to underscore the fact that designing with an emphasis on *contribution*, rather than pure content, can foster *even more* engaged, motivated, and successful learners.

But what exactly does "designing for contribution" encompass? It involves creating space within the learning process for students to be more than just receivers of information; it involves enabling them to be dynamic participants. One approach to designing for contribution is crafting opportunities for students to engage with each other during direct instruction. These might take the form of brainstorming

103

sessions, think-pair-share activities, or group discussions. Such activities encourage students to exchange ideas, perspectives, and opinions with their peers, thereby rendering their learning a more collaborative and engaging process. By fostering connections between new content and students' prior knowledge and experiences, we can enhance their engagement with the material and bolster their understanding of the presented concepts.

To render your direct instruction more captivating and involve students more deeply, consider these strategies I've found particularly effective:

Use polling during the presentation. Utilize digital tools like Nearpod, Kahoot, Mentimeter, or Poll Everywhere to create polls relevant to the content being presented. For instance, during a history lesson on the Civil War, you might poll students on what they believe was the most significant factor leading to the conflict. This not only encourages student participation but also introduces diverse perspectives into the discussion.

Collaborative note-taking. Instead of delivering a monologue, involve students in the note-taking process. With a shared Google Doc or another collaborative tool, ask students to summarize key points or contribute their own insights as the presentation unfolds.

Interactive media. Incorporate videos or other interactive media to make presentations more engaging. Include a video clip of an expert discussing a new scientific discovery, or a simulation that allows students to virtually explore an important historical site.

Reflection and discussion. Foster reflection and discussion both during and after the presentation. Ask students to consider their learning, sharing any lingering questions, or exploring how they might apply the content to their own lives. These reflective discussions can occur in pairs, small groups, or as a whole class.

The following story of Ethan, a 9th grade Biology student, is a poignant illustration of the transformative power of this approach:

From Passive Listener to Active Participant

In Mr. Maldonado's biology class, the conventional approach had been a teacher-centric one where students were mostly relegated to passive listening roles. A clear indicator of this dynamic was Ethan, a student who seemed disinterested in the classroom proceedings. Whether he was doodling on his notebook or gazing blankly during lectures, it was apparent that the traditional teaching methods weren't engaging him. His lackluster performance and unenthusiastic attitude towards biology became a concern for Mr. Maldonado, who sought to change the learning atmosphere.

Mr. Maldonado realized that a shift towards a more interactive and engaging approach was required to spark interest in students like Ethan. He decided to incorporate brainstorming sessions and group discussions into his lectures. This transition wasn't immediate. Mr. Maldonado first introduced a brainstorming session as an experiment. The idea was to discuss the concept of cell division with students and encourage them to share their ideas and questions. Initially, the students were hesitant, including Ethan, but as they grew more comfortable with the new format, they began participating more actively.

Over the next few weeks, Mr. Maldonado introduced group discussions. He divided the class into small groups, assigned them specific topics, and provided them with guiding questions. Each group was responsible for researching their topic, discussing it amongst themselves, and presenting their findings to the class.

The change in Ethan was gradual but noticeable. At first, he was quiet during group activities, but he gradually started contributing more. Mr. Maldonado also noticed that Ethan was doodling less during classes and started making more biology-related notes. Over time, Ethan's questions during group discussions grew more insightful and his contributions more frequent.

By the end of the semester, Ethan was a completely different student in biology class. His participation was enthusiastic and consistent, and he often led his group in discussions and presentations. His improvement was not only noticeable in his attitude but also in his grades. The mid-term report showed a significant improvement in his biology grades and feedback from his peers showed a noticeable increase in his confidence.

Transforming a classroom environment from passive to active learning isn't an overnight endeavor. It requires strategic planning, consistent efforts, and a flexible approach to teaching. But it's my hope that using the example of Mr. Maldonado, it underlined that when given the chance and the right environment, every student, even those like Ethan who seem disengaged, can become active contributors to the learning process. Such strategic changes in teaching methods can

> Transforming a classroom environment from passive to active learning isn't an overnight endeavor. It requires strategic planning, consistent efforts, and a flexible approach to teaching.

help spark enthusiasm, improve understanding, and boost overall academic performance.

The journey from passive consumption to active contribution in the learning process, however, is not confined to instructional strategies alone. The physical environment of the classroom plays a vital role in shaping this transformation. Just as we've explored how to engage students through interactive presentations, group discussions, and reflective practices, we must also recognize that the very layout of our classrooms can either foster or hinder these efforts.

The design of the learning space is not merely a backdrop; it's an active participant in the educational process. As we transition to the next section, we'll look at ways in which the physical room layout can be strategically used to create connections, enhance collaboration, and *Effectively Design Instruction*. By aligning the physical space with our educational philosophy, we can create a cohesive environment that supports our goal of turning every student from a passive listener to an active participant in their learning journey.

EDI Strategy: Using the Physical Room Layout to Create Connections

Studies show that the physical design of a classroom can significantly influence student engagement, behavior, and academic achievement. A thoughtfully designed classroom can stimulate a positive learning environment, fostering collaboration, creativity, and critical thinking. Conversely, an ill-designed classroom may lead to distractions, disengagement, or even disruptive behavior.

As an educator, you may not have full control over the physical layout of your classroom. However, you can strategically utilize existing fixtures and fittings. Once you've arranged the student desks, standing workstations, bean bags, and other unconventional seating options, your next focus should be on who sits where.

Your decisions should be informed by your teaching style, the nature of the learning activity, and your objectives. Environmental psychologist Robert Sommer once stated that a teacher's educational philosophy is mirrored in the classroom layout. Thus, every desk and chair arrangement should align with specific educational goals. As stated in this book's introduction, there's no one-size-fits-all classroom layout for all activities, much like there's no universal airplane cockpit.

To illustrate, let's turn our attention to Mrs. Van Kirk, an 11th-grade Physics teacher. Like Mr. Maldonado, she too was determined to *Effectively Design Instruction* for her students. She noticed students seated at the back were less likely to participate and often seemed disengaged. Furthermore, during group projects, a few voices often dominated the discussions, while quieter students barely contributed. Inspired by the research on the impact of classroom layout on student engagement, Mrs. Van Kirk decided to experiment.

She carefully considered her teaching style and the nature of her lessons which included lectures, group work, and individual activities. She transitioned from desks grouped in traditional rows to a semi-circular layout which allowed eye contact with each student during lectures. For group activities, she organized smaller "pods," fostering more equal participation. She also ensured a clear line of sight to the board for each student and minimized distractions such as screen glare and physical obstructions.

The impact was immediately noticeable. Students who had previously been reticent started asking questions and contributing more to group discussions. Class behaviors improved, and the classroom energy shifted to being more dynamic and vibrant.

According to Yale University, the set-up of the classroom space can shape teacher pedagogy, choice of activities, and on-task student behavior. For example, a classroom with traditional seating in rows directed toward the front of the room results in teachers spending more time in lecture and students demonstrating less active engagement. In contrast, roundtable seating arrangements lead to instructors and students engaging in more active learning activities.

Here are six options for classroom seating arrangements taken from Yale University's Center for Teaching and Learning. For more of an explanation on each configuration, visit https://poorvucenter.yale.edu/ClassroomSeatingArrangements.

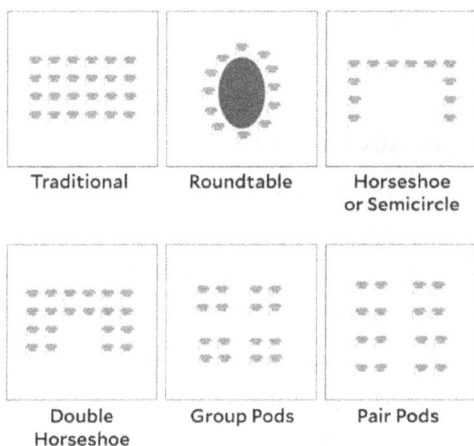

| Traditional | Roundtable | Horseshoe or Semicircle |
| Double Horseshoe | Group Pods | Pair Pods |

In the end, the best classroom layout is the one that aligns with your teaching context, students' needs, and the learning goals at that specific time. By being mindful of your educational philosophy and teaching style, you can design a classroom layout that encourages engagement, supports diverse learning activities, and fosters an inclusive, equitable learning environment. Much like Mr. Maldonado's class, by thoughtfully using the physical room layout, you can create an environment that invites active student contribution, participation, and learning.

Appearance Does Matter

When I assumed the role of Director of Technology, I walked into a scenario familiar to many districts: Garnet Valley's technology infrastructure consisted primarily of classroom iPad carts and a computer lab in every school. These labs were designed in a standard format, with desktop computers arranged around the room's periphery. However, with the shift towards one-to-one devices, the need for these traditional labs decreased, and the demand for flexible instructional spaces grew.

The solution? Transforming these spaces into Collaborative and Innovation (C&I) Labs, Garnet Valley's unique version of Makerspaces. These new labs featured flexible seating arrangements and desks, cutting-edge technology like 3D printers and robots, and even play-based learning tools such as Lego and Hot Wheel kits. The transition wasn't always easy—budget constraints meant we often had to create shelving and stencils by hand. Our instructional coaches at the time, Mrs. Julie Devine, Mrs. Janine Conley, and Mr. Mike Simone, led a team of teacher volunteers to overhaul the spaces, replacing carpets, demolishing shelving, and repainting walls.

The success of the C&I Labs soon permeated the rest of our schools, with classrooms quickly adopting flexible seating and more dynamic layouts. Despite the disruption caused by the pandemic, we remained committed to creating learning environments that cater to diverse student needs, both physically and digitally. As we move forward, we aim to regain our pre-pandemic momentum by re-evaluating and updating our learning spaces to meet our students' evolving needs.

Just as we meticulously plan the physical layout of our classrooms to create an engaging and inclusive atmosphere, we must bring that same diligence and creativity to the digital landscape. An appealing, well-structured digital presentation can elevate the learning experience, facilitate better understanding, and boost student engagement. So, let's dive deeper into how we can make our digital presentations as appealing and effective as our physical classrooms.

EDI Strategy: Digital Page Layout–Simple, but Not Simplistic

Our journey from conventional classrooms to innovative, engaging learning spaces has taught us many valuable lessons. These lessons extend beyond the confines of our physical classrooms and into our digital ones. One way we help teachers to apply new learning is by focusing our collective efforts on digital page layout. A well-designed LMS layout can significantly enhance student learning experiences and outcomes. However, just like in our physical classrooms, our digital designs should be simple, but not simplistic.

To illustrate this, consider the two presentations below on pollution caused by the fishing industry. The first uses a standard Power-Point template, complete with clip art. The second takes a minimalist approach, with a creative commons image and a straightforward text box.

Before

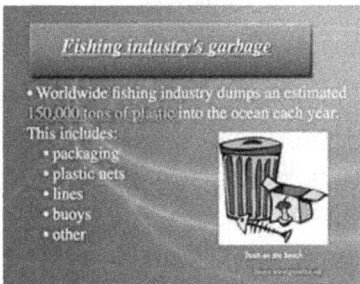

After

When looking at the images, it becomes clear that the second presentation is more likely to capture the audience's attention and communicate a stronger message. Thankfully, there are numerous platforms available, such as Adobe and Canva, that can assist teachers in crafting visually engaging content. But in this digital arena, remember to respect copyright laws and be mindful of the accessibility needs of your students when creating images for your presentations.

One key aspect of effective digital page layout is consistency. A consistent design not only communicates professionalism but also makes the content more digestible for your audience. When working with new teachers, I find the following three areas a good place to focus:

Fonts: Use one style for headings and another for body text, with the option of a third for decorative elements such as large titles or divider pages.

Colors: Choose a few colors for your presentation and maintain them throughout. Consider how the colors of your slides and backgrounds can set the mood and tone of your content.

Design Elements: Ensure that photographs, icons, and other visuals maintain a cohesive style across the presentation.

In the same way that we wouldn't rely on a one-size-fits-all layout for our physical classrooms, we mustn't depend on generic templates found in PowerPoint or Google Slides for our digital presentations. By applying the strategies above, you can ensure that your digital learning environment mirrors the engagement and deep understanding we strive to promote in our physical classrooms.

Winning the Battle for Your Students' and Parents' Attention

Our students' worlds are inextricably linked with technology. Their interactions, amusement, and education are predominantly mediated through digital platforms. With the emergence of smartphones, tablets, and other digital devices, we've seen a seismic shift in traditional educational paradigms. This evolution compels us to adapt and innovate our content delivery methods to meet the changing ways in which students engage.

The digitization of learning has brought a wealth of knowledge to our students' fingertips. Thanks to the internet, students can now delve into a myriad of topics that were once inaccessible, fostering a deeper understanding and broadening their horizons. Classroom interactions have broken free of physical limitations, as technology bridges the gap, connecting students to both peers and educators across the globe. However, these very advancements bring with them a multitude of digital distractions, which have been shown to have a considerable impact on students' attention spans and focus. Various studies have shown a correlation between the use of digital devices and reduced attention span, a challenge that traditional learning environments must navigate, particularly during activities requiring sustained concentration.

To tackle this issue, we need to bridge the gap between traditional teaching methods and the modern, interactive way students now engage with information. Let's consider Mrs. Reid, a middle school librarian in Maryland, who used an innovative approach to capture her students' interest during library lessons. She incorporated an augmented reality (AR) app on her students' iPads, transforming reading material into an immersive, visually captivating experience. This innovative approach seized her students' attention and nurtured a more active learning environment, bolstering their comprehension and stimulating creativity.

Similarly, Mr. Jackson, a high school English teacher, chose to exchange traditional lecture-style teaching for a flipped classroom model. This approach introduces new content online—often via video lectures—before class, reserving class time for exercises, projects, or discussions to encourage the understanding and application of this knowledge. By shifting lectures to homework, Mr. Jackson used class time for collaborative discussions, group projects, and creative writing exercises.

The active learning models employed by Mrs. Reid and Mr. Jackson not only invigorated their students' comprehension of complex topics but also allowed for deeper exploration of ideas and fostered a richer understanding of the content. From these examples, it becomes clear that innovative teaching methods have the power to enhance content delivery and meet our students' diverse needs. By designing engaging, interactive learning experiences, we not only foster inclusivity and encourage active participation but, most importantly, put our students at the center of their learning journey.

As educators navigating an ever-evolving landscape, we must continually adapt our content presentation methods. Incorporating multimedia tools, AR, virtual reality, game-based learning, and flipped classrooms can create a dynamic learning environment that promotes academic success while nurturing students' overall well-being.

As we explore innovative strategies to win our students' attention in the classroom, we must recognize that our responsibility extends beyond the school walls. The digital era has not only transformed the way students engage with learning but also how parents interact with the educational process. The same principles that guide us in creating engaging, interactive learning experiences for our students can be applied to foster a deeper connection with their parents.

In the next section, we will dive into the essential aspect of nurturing parental engagement, particularly in a technology-driven educational landscape. By understanding and empathizing with parents' experiences and perspectives, we can create a more inclusive and supportive learning environment that benefits not only our students but their families as well. This holistic approach ensures that we are not only capturing the attention of our students but also building bridges with their parents and fosters a collaborative educational community that thrives on empathy, understanding, and shared goals.

EDI Strategy: Nurturing Parental Engagement through Empathy Mapping

As we navigate our day-to-day responsibilities, it can be easy to overlook that we serve multiple audiences in our role as educators. Notably, parents, who may be unfamiliar with the technology deployed in our classrooms, form a critical part of our educational community. Remember, many parents find the digital tools and resources we use intimidating. Their own schooling experiences likely didn't involve the same technology, and this unfamiliarity might leave them feeling ill-equipped to effectively support their child's learning.

Understanding and empathizing with our students' parents is paramount. It's important to acknowledge that they might be feeling overwhelmed and uncertain about how best to assist their children. But it's equally crucial to remember that everyone starts somewhere. As educators, we can empower parents by offering resources and support, such as a parent toolkit or dedicated parent folder within the LMS.

In this parent toolkit, teachers can include materials such as tutorials or guides on using the LMS, details about specific features and tools available within the system for parents, and tips on leveraging the LMS to communicate with teachers. Nowadays, many LMS platforms already offer resources to guide parents on navigating the system. Depending on the specific platform, numerous features and tools are available to assist parents in overcoming any initial technology hurdles.

Investing time in understanding and supporting parents new to technology can profoundly enhance the personalized learning experience for our students, and indeed, their parents. To effectively encapsulate the parental perspective while designing and delivering instruction via your LMS, I recommend creating a Parent Empathy Map, similar to the one below that I use when working with new teachers.

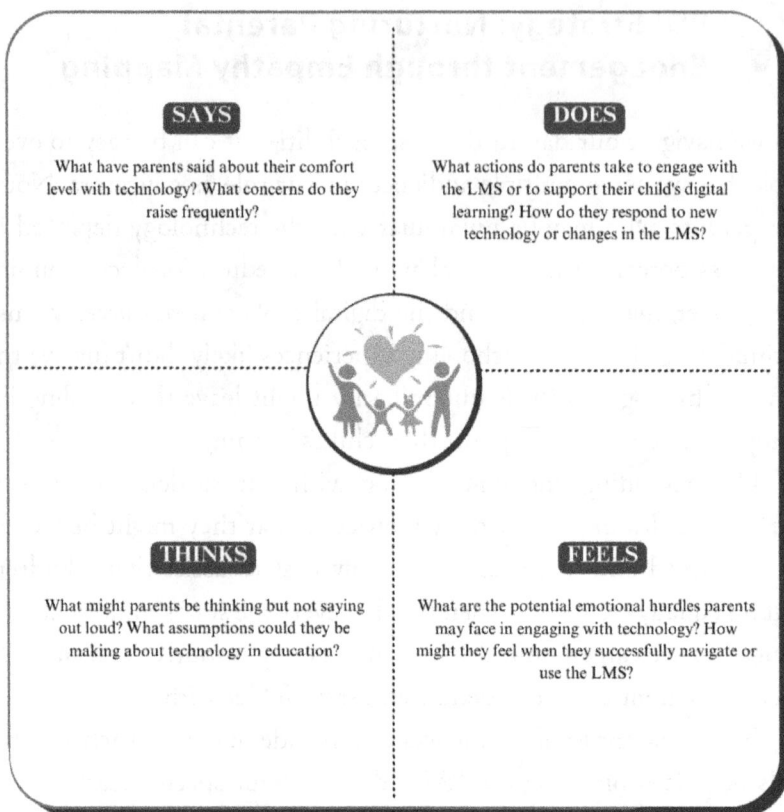

Empathy Maps are typically divided into four quadrants: "Says," "Thinks," "Does," and "Feels." Let's look closer at each section:

Says. This quadrant captures what parents may publicly express about their experiences using the LMS. To fill this section out, I encourage teachers to consider feedback gathered from parent-teacher meetings, comments made during school events, or inputs collected through surveys. Questions to consider might include: What have parents said about their comfort level with technology? What concerns do they raise frequently?

116

Thinks. This section dives into the internal dialogues or thoughts of the parents. While this information may not always be publicly shared, it's essential for teachers to empathize with what parents might be contemplating or worrying about. Some guiding questions might be: What might parents be thinking, but not saying out loud? What assumptions could they be making about technology in education?

Does. Here, the focus is on the actions parents take related to the LMS and digital learning. This can be captured through observing their engagement with the platform, their response to requests for involvement, or their application of resources provided. Questions might include: What actions do parents take to engage with the LMS or to support their child's digital learning? How do they respond to new technology or changes in the LMS?

Feels. In this quadrant, explore the emotional responses parents might have towards the LMS and digital learning. Teachers should consider any anxieties, frustrations, or positive emotions parents may feel. Helpful questions may include: What are the potential emotional hurdles parents may face in engaging with technology? How might they feel when they use the LMS?

Creating an Empathy Map serves as an impactful way to understand the viewpoint of parents unfamiliar with using an LMS. This approach enables teachers to explore the thoughts, feelings, and experiences of parents, and subsequently, design and deliver instruction that aligns with their needs and bolsters their child's learning.

Utilizing an Empathy Map offers several advantages. It allows teachers to view the class from the parents' perspective. This insight can guide teachers in creating more personalized, supportive instruction for parents unfamiliar with technology. It can also help to identify previously unconsidered pain points. For example, parents may struggle to locate certain resources they need to support their child's learning. Armed with this knowledge, teachers can better label folders and support mechanisms to address these pain points and foster the gains that parents are seeking.

Utilizing an Empathy Map can also help foster stronger relationships with parents. A deeper understanding of their experiences can facilitate more effective communication and provide the support they need to better contribute to their child's education. It can lead to improved student outcomes and bolster relationships with parents. By deeply understanding the parent perspective, teachers can design and deliver instruction that effectively meets their needs and aids their child's learning.

Empowering Students with "Futuristic" Technologies

When I envision technology in the classroom, the image of students using tablets or laptops for note-taking, research, and presentations comes to mind. However, with the emergence of cutting-edge technologies like virtual and augmented reality (VR & AR) and wearable, interconnected devices such as smartwatches, we find ourselves on the brink of experiencing a classroom that bears a striking resemblance to the futuristic world of *The Jetsons*. Embracing these cutting-edge technologies can provide teachers with the support and guidance needed to navigate today's rapidly evolving educational landscape.

For those who didn't grow up eagerly awaiting Saturday morning cartoons, *The Jetsons* was a beloved cartoon set in 2062 that chronicled the life of a futuristic family living in a highly automated world teeming with extraordinary inventions. The Jetsons—George, Jane, Judy, Elroy, and their robot maid Rosie—enjoyed a life of leisure and convenience, thanks to cutting-edge technologies like flying cars, jetpacks, instant meal machines, holographic telephones, moving sidewalks, and even a robot dog.

Back in the 1960s, when the show first aired, the Jetsons' world seemed like a distant fantasy. Fast-forward to today, and we find ourselves on the cusp of some of the groundbreaking technologies showcased in the show, such as autonomous vehicles, household robots, and space travel. What once appeared far-fetched is now becoming reality, and making an impact on all aspects of our lives, including education.

In the previous section, you read how Mrs. Reid uses VR to maximize student agency and inclusivity, grabbing the attention of her middle school students who tend to zone out during library class. However, these immersive technologies aren't merely attention-grabbers. When thoughtfully integrated into lessons, they enable students to virtually travel back in time to witness historical events or explore literary settings in a more intimate and personal way. While these tools may seem costly and inaccessible, affordable options like Google Cardboard are making virtual and augmented reality experiences increasingly attainable for all schools.

Additionally, everyday technologies like smartwatches and fitness trackers can also be harnessed to create dynamic, immersive lessons. Consider Mr. Lee, an innovative teacher who leverages his students' smartwatches to *Effectively Design Instruction* by teaching his students about the cardiovascular system and the importance of exercise.

In his lesson plan on the cardiovascular system, Mr. Lee, a Health/ PE teacher in Bergen County, New Jersey, sets up a practical, hands-on activity for his students. First, he teaches them about heart rate and how it's affected by various factors, such as physical activity and stress. Then, he has the students pair up and use their smartwatches to measure their resting heart rate. After recording their baseline measurements, the students engage in a series of exercises designed to increase their heart rate, such as jumping jacks, running in place, and push-ups.

Throughout the activity, the students monitor their heart rate on their smartwatches, observing the changes as they exercise. This real-time feedback not only helps students grasp the concept of cardiovascular health, but also allows them to see the direct impact of exercise on their bodies.

Following the activity, Mr. Lee leads a discussion in which students share their observations and reflect on the importance of regular exercise for maintaining a healthy cardiovascular system. By intentionally integrating smartwatches into his lesson plan, Mr. Lee leverages the technology his students already own and better personalizes the learning experience by making it more meaningful for his students.

As we continue to embrace these technologies and others, we can create more engaging and meaningful learning environments for students. By incorporating these new technologies into our lesson planning, we can foster more personalized learning experiences, allowing students to explore content at their own pace and in their own way.

The world of *The Jetsons* may not be as far away as it once seemed. As technology continues to advance and integrate seamlessly into our daily lives, we must adapt and find creative ways to incorporate these tools into our classrooms. By doing so, we can create engaging, inclusive learning environments that maximize student agency and foster a deeper understanding of the subject matter.

For educators, the benefits of embracing these technologies are numerous. Teachers can save time, improve lesson planning, and better assess student understanding by using tools like VR, AR, and smartwatches in their teaching practice. By leveraging technology effectively, teachers can not only enhance their instruction but also better support and guide students in their learning journeys.

As we move forward in the 21st century, it is crucial for educators to continue exploring and integrating new technologies into their teaching practices. By doing so, we can bridge the gap between 1962 and 2062, and help our students navigate a rapidly changing world. The future of education is already here, and it's more thrilling than we ever imagined.

EDI Strategy: Being a Curator, not a Dumper

As we increasingly embrace the Jetsons-like era of educational technology, we must strike a balance between leveraging these powerful resources and ensuring our students are not overwhelmed. This brings us to a critical strategy in digital-age teaching: being a curator rather than a dumper.

> I would be remiss if I didn't express my profound gratitude to Dr. Adam Lavellee, Bonnie Lathram, and others at Global Online Academy (GOA), whose insights were instrumental in my understanding of the concept of *intentional* instructional design and the importance of curation in online and blended learning. When our team had the privilege of working with GOA, their articulation of this concept had a significant impact on us. Their approach broadened our perspective and emphasized how much we still had to explore in the realm of online and blended learning. Adam and Bonnie, your invaluable insights continue to shape my approach to digital-age teaching and for that, I am truly grateful.

In this era of abundant online resources, it's tempting for educators, particularly those new to digital learning platforms, to flood their LMS pages with a plethora of content. The intention, of course, is to offer students a vast array of resources to facilitate their learning. However, this well-intentioned strategy can inadvertently create a disorganized learning landscape, paradoxically obstructing student engagement. Even more challenging, this approach can be particularly discouraging for students with limited executive functioning skills, making them feel overwhelmed to the point of surrender.

Platforms like Schoology, Canvas, and Google Classroom are central hubs for resource sharing, communication, and progress tracking, and thoughtful curation is key for creating an optimal learning experience. Educational blogger and podcaster Jennifer Gonzalez defines curation as selecting and organizing resources meaningfully and relevantly for learners. If you do not already, I strongly recommend following Jennifer and becoming a subscriber to her podcast *Cult of Pedagogy*.

The benefits of curating resources in an LMS include focusing on important and relevant materials, preventing information overload and enhancing student engagement and retention. Curating also creates a cohesive and structured learning experience by organizing materials logically and intuitively, and allows for tailoring the learning experience to meet specific student needs and interests by aligning resources with course goals and objectives.

With the increasing volume of online information, teachers now face the difficult task to find, verify, organize, annotate, remix, create, collate, and share resources that excite, inspire, and fuel students' passion for learning. Jennifer Gonzalez's work on becoming expert curators can help teachers become better curators. This is especially important at the elementary level because primary students tend to be less self-sufficient.

This emphasis on curation brings to mind Mrs. Emma Jordan, an elementary school teacher who I first met through a Twitter Chat. In her early enthusiasm to leverage technology, Emma overloaded her LMS with resources. This over-abundance of materials inadvertently created a barrier to learning, as students like Jada struggled to navigate the deluge of content.

Confronted by Jada's frustration, Emma realized that her approach, though well-intentioned, was stifling rather than stimulating learning. This realization sparked a transformation in her method, guiding her to become a more deliberate curator of resources. She began by trimming the materials to only the most relevant, organized them with purpose, and added context to each resource. This facilitated her students' and their parents' navigation, leading to an improvement in engagement and understanding.

Mrs. Jordan's journey underlines the necessity of careful curation to create an effective learning environment in this new world of educational technology. As we travel further into the exciting realm of future technologies, our task as educators is not just to present these technologies to our students, but to guide them through the landscape thoughtfully. We need to ensure that in our pursuit to create the classroom of *The Jetsons*, we remember the need for simplicity and clarity. We must balance our fascination with the future against our commitment to creating engaging, inclusive, and personalized learning environments that our students can readily navigate and benefit from.

Amplifying Your Voice in the LMS

Beyond merely serving as a repository for assignments and resources, an LMS can become a digital megaphone, amplifying a teacher's voice and enhancing their presence in both the physical and virtual classroom. This amplified voice can promote interaction, design engaging learning experiences, and foster student agency and inclusivity.

In a traditional classroom, students must rely on their memory for instructions and content delivery. However, an LMS allows teachers to record these key points of instruction, providing learners the ability to revisit and reflect on their learning at their own pace. This capability amplifies teachers' instruction and feedback and can greatly enhance their impact on students.

Consider the example of a teacher explaining a complex topic in a video and posting it to the LMS. This video can be replayed by students as many times as they need to fully comprehend the subject matter, providing additional support for those who may have initially struggled with the concept. This also extends to feedback on assignments. Rather than providing feedback in the traditional form of written comments, teachers can opt for audio or video comments to offer in-depth, personalized critique, giving students a clear roadmap for improving their work.

Take the story of Mr. Goldberg, a teacher who successfully harnessed the power of an LMS to create engaging and accessible content, and thereby promoted student agency and inclusivity for his students. By injecting his personality and humor into the instructional videos he uploaded onto the LMS, Mr. Goldberg created a vibrant virtual classroom that actively engaged his students in their learning journey.

Under the guise of "Scribe Goldberg," he used his virtual platform to bring the history of ancient Egypt to life. His narrative covered the critical role of the Nile River, the process of mummification, and the civilization's art, architecture, and mythology. His vivid use of visuals and props created an immersive learning experience, and his persona made his voice resonate even more strongly within the LMS.

Mr. Goldberg also created discussion boards within the LMS, fostering a collaborative space for students to ask questions, share insights, and connect with their peers. His active participation in these discussions enabled him to address individual student needs and offer personalized feedback.

Embracing the potential of an LMS to amplify teachers' voices and make content engaging and accessible can empower students with agency and inclusivity in their learning. By viewing the LMS as an integral part of instructional design rather than an optional add-on, educators can harness its full potential and effectively support student success in today's ever-evolving educational landscape.

EDI Strategy: Crafting Your Own Instructional Videos

The integration of video in classroom instruction brings a multitude of benefits for both teachers and students. These benefits span from the saved time in delivering new concepts, to forging genuine connections with students and their families. The positive impacts of utilizing video are tangible, often resulting in improved test scores, increased interaction with learning material, and a deepened understanding of subjects. As a strategy to capture and sustain student interest, video integration in lessons is second to none.

Yet, for many educators, even tech-savvy ones, the process of creating videos can appear formidable. The idea of being on screen might be nerve-wracking, and the technical aspects of shooting and editing videos could seem like Herculean tasks. While there's no substitute for hands-on experience, certain key guidelines can simplify the process. Essential tips include preparing a detailed script, choosing a quiet location for recording, identifying the best recording tools, and ensuring the videos are short enough to suit the target age group:

Scripting for Success. Crafting a well-thought-out script ensures that key points aren't overlooked, helps prevent rambling, and maintains pacing in line with the video's rhythm. A script also facilitates concise and coherent instruction, fostering better understanding and retention of content by students.

Choosing the Ideal Recording Environment. The room in which you record is crucial to the overall quality of your video. Opt for a quiet, distraction-free space where potential interruptions from pets or other people are minimized. Rooms with carpeting or furnishings that can absorb sound are ideal for reducing echo and enhancing audio quality.

Prioritize Quality Audio. Investing in a good microphone is essential for capturing clear and crisp audio. Even with the best content, poor audio quality can make a video difficult to follow, and ultimately hamper the learning process.

Find a Tool You Like. There's an array of both free and paid tools available to assist you in crafting your videos. These tools often come with features that let you incorporate scripts, images, shapes, music, school branding, and more.

Keep Them Short. Although the perfect length for a video depends on the content and target audience, a good rule of thumb is to strive for videos of no more than three minutes. Short, focused videos are more digestible, maintain attention, and increase the chances of students revisiting the content for reinforcement.

The ideal length of a video is a frequently asked question. While the appropriate duration depends on the content and audience, I generally recommend keeping videos under three minutes, if feasible. For teachers with extensive content, I advocate for creating several concise videos instead of a single lengthy one.

While sourcing suitable videos online is certainly acceptable, my experience has proven that teacher-created instructional videos have a more profound impact on students. A compelling example of this is the story of Mr. Rudy Shiller, a Probability and Statistics teacher at Garnet Valley High School.

Mr. Shiller is renowned for his innovative teaching methods, which consistently engage students and make his Probability and Statistics course a top choice. Mr. Shiller exemplifies the principle of *Effectively Designed Instruction* for his students. He shared that, despite the professionally produced Khan Academy and YouTube videos featured in his course, his students preferred his self-created videos. This preference stemmed from the familiarity and comfort students found in their teacher's style, voice, and mannerisms, which seemed to boost their engagement and retention.

While it isn't always feasible to produce videos for every lesson, Mr. Shiller's personalized videos aligned seamlessly with the district curriculum and fostered a cohesive learning experience. Additionally, creating his own instructional videos allowed Mr. Shiller to incorporate real-world examples, add more local contexts and school-specific references, and make the material more relatable and captivating for his students.

Reflecting on Presenting Content

Crafting engaging, inclusive, and effective lessons require thoughtful planning and a reflective approach to content presentation. As we journeyed through this chapter, we have discovered a wealth of techniques and strategies to enhance the delivery of your content and create the most dynamic, accessible, and enriching learning experiences for your students.

Throughout our exploration of the six EDI Strategies for Presenting Content, we've unveiled the profound influence of storytelling as a captivating medium for learners, offering a bridge of connection to the subject matter. We've addressed the importance of utilizing diverse media formats—such as videos, podcasts, and interactive games—as vehicles to resonate with students of differing learning styles and preferences.

This chapter also underscored the benefits of interweaving culturally responsive teaching into your lesson designs, promoting equity and inclusion by acknowledging and honoring the rich tapestry of your students' backgrounds and experiences. Coupled with this, we've also recognized the transformative potential of integrating real-world examples and problem-solving tasks which can empower students to deploy their newly acquired knowledge and skills within practical contexts.

It is my hope that the EDI Strategies for Presenting Content inspire you to think both critically and innovatively about your teaching approach to ensure your lessons resonate with each individual learner and cultivating a learning environment conducive to every student's growth and success.

As you ponder the information and insights shared in this chapter, I invite you to reflect on the following guiding questions:

1. How can you intentionally design your presentations to prioritize accessibility, as exemplified by Pierre du Pont's vision of Longwood Gardens?
2. Drawing inspiration from Mrs. Reid's example of incorporating VR in her library, how might you integrate more hands-on activities to transform your students from passive observers to active learners?
3. What steps can you take to prioritize "designing for student contribution" over just content, to encourage students like Ethan to engage more actively?
4. In the vein of Mr. Lee's use of everyday technologies like smartwatches and fitness trackers in his Health/PE classes, how might you leverage similar tools to render your lessons more dynamic and authentic?
5. How can you amplify your voice in the LMS in a way that resonates with your students, as "Scribe Goldberg" so effectively did with his students?
6. How can you ensure your unique voice and personality shine through in your LMS, effectively bridging the digital divide between you and your students?

CHAPTER IV

~

EDI Theme: Accessibility & Inclusion

"There are no labels in UDL. There are only fabulous, amazing students with different levels of variability."

–Katie Novak

Imagine for a moment the untapped potential waiting to be discovered within the walls of your classroom. Among your students there are sure to be hidden talents, creative visionaries, and future leaders whose abilities are not yet fully recognized. For millions of students across the country, accessibility and inclusion are vital to unleashing their true capabilities.

As we set out to explore this vital subject, let's briefly pause to outline the journey ahead in this chapter:

EDI Focus	Benefits to Students	Try It Out
Using the POUR Principles for Accessible Materials	Implementing the POUR Principal for materials ensures that students of all abilities can interact with content.	Creating Perceivable, Operable, Understandable, and Robust materials (p. 134)
Address Learner Variability by Digitizing Resources	Digitizing resources allows for easy adaptation and customization to individual needs.	Planning for predictable barriers in your classroom (p. 137)
Ensuring Multiple Means of Action & Expression	By offering various ways for students to demonstrate their understanding, this approach acknowledges that there is no "one-size-fits-all" method for expression.	Actionable steps to ensure students have multiple opportunities to express their learning (p. 144)
Ensuring Multiple Means of Engagement	By offering different ways to capture students' interest and motivation, educators can tap into diverse passions and inspire deeper connections to the material.	Three ways to provide Multiple Means of Engagement (p. 147)

EDI Focus	Benefits to Students	Try It Out
Ensuring Multiple Means of Representation	By offering information in various formats (e.g., visual, auditory, tactile), educators can cater to diverse learning styles.	Six ways to provide for Multiple Means of Representation (p. 150)
Applying Accommodations and Modification	This strategy recognizes individual challenges and strengths, fostering an inclusive environment that encourages growth and success	Strategies to apply accommodations and modification (p. 154)

As an educator today, you play a crucial role in fostering an inclusive and accessible learning environment for all your students. Regardless of the challenges they face, each student has unique strengths and deserves the opportunity to succeed. In this chapter, we'll probe the world of accessibility and inclusion in our schools, exploring the strategies, tools, and mindsets required to empower every learner.

This chapter is more than a guide; it's an invitation to transformation. Whether you're a seasoned educator or just beginning your journey, the insights shared here equip you to create classrooms that resonate with every learner. It's a call to action for *Effectively Designed Instruction*, to harness the principles of Universal Design for Learning (UDL), and to champion a revolution in education where inclusivity isn't just a buzzword but the heartbeat of your classroom. Join us as we take this vital step towards a future where every student is empowered to reach their full, extraordinary potential.

Yes, All Really Does Mean Everyone

In every role I've played—as a parent, coach, or educator—I have passionately believed that education should be an empowering force that caters to each student, regardless of their academic abilities or unique needs. Yet, like many, I've faced challenges in realizing this ideal.

Accessibility and inclusion aren't just buzzwords or legal obligations; they are the essence of quality education. While we often focus on students with recognized needs, such as those with an IEP or 504 plan, the reality is that every student benefits from inclusivity.

> Accessibility and inclusion aren't just buzzwords or legal obligations; they are the essence of quality education.

Take the story of Project Access at Adlai E. Stevenson High School, a program initially designed for students with learning disabilities like dyslexia. Here, the impact went beyond the intended audience. Teachers began to embrace Universal Design for Learning (UDL) principles, a framework that recognizes the uniqueness of each learner and offers multiple ways of engaging with content.

Universal Design for Learning (UDL) is an educational approach that emphasizes flexibility, customization, and inclusivity. It is based on three main principles:

Multiple Means of Representation. This principle encourages teachers to present information in various ways, such as through text, visual aids, audio, or interactive methods. It recognizes that different students perceive and comprehend information differently, so providing alternatives enhances understanding.

Multiple Means of Action and Expression. This acknowledges that students have diverse ways of interacting with content and demonstrating their knowledge. By providing different options for expression, like writing, speaking, or creating visual projects, teachers enable students to show their understanding in ways that suit their strengths.

Multiple Means of Engagement. Recognizing that students' interests and motivations vary, this principle promotes offering choices and challenges that engage them. Whether through collaborative projects, individualized learning paths, or connecting content to real-world applications, providing different ways to engage helps maintain interest and motivation.

The implementation of UDL principles at Stevenson High School led to the use of multimedia resources, alternative text formats, and flexible assessment options. The ripple effect was astonishing—the entire student body, not just those with learning disabilities, began to flourish. The approach made learning more engaging, motivating, and successful for all students. The unexpected consequence? Stevenson High School's academic performance and graduation rates improved significantly! Teachers reported increased student participation, enhanced focus, and a stronger sense of community within the classrooms. The accommodations and support initially provided for students like Steven through Project Access had inadvertently created a more accessible and inclusive learning environment for all.

The success of Project Access caught the attention of educators and experts nationwide which led to its adoption by other schools across the country. Today, Adlai E. Stevenson High School is recognized as a leader in inclusive education and serves as a model for implementing effective accommodations and support for students with special education needs.

Steven's story and the success of Project Access at Stevenson High School illustrate the power of accessibility and inclusion in education. By addressing the needs of students with special education requirements, schools can create an environment where every student has an equal opportunity to succeed, ultimately benefiting the entire student body.

This isn't just a success story of one school. It's a lesson for all educators that an accessible and inclusive learning environment isn't merely beneficial, but essential, for every student to reach their full potential.

So, let's commit together to shape the lives and futures of those we teach, ensuring that every student, regardless of their unique needs and circumstances, has the opportunity to thrive and succeed.

🔆 EDI Strategy: Using the POUR Principles for Accessible Materials

Creating accessible materials can feel daunting, but it doesn't have to be. The POUR principles, taken from the Web Content Accessibility Guidelines 2.1 (2018), offer an excellent roadmap to design content that's accessible to all students. The POUR principles stand for **Perceivable, Operable, Understandable, and Robust.** These four qualities help create an accessible experience that caters to a diverse range of learning needs. By integrating these principles into your instructional design, you can ensure that your content is accessible to students with various abilities and learning preferences, and promote an inclusive environment in which everyone can thrive.

To design with accessibility in mind, it's good practice to start by making your content **Perceivable.** This means presenting information in multiple formats, such as text, images, and audio, to accommodate different learning styles. For example, when sharing a video, consider providing captions, transcripts, or audio descriptions so that students with hearing impairments can access the content. Likewise, use clear and concise language, and consider incorporating alternative text for images to support students with visual impairments.

Next, ensure that your content is **Operable**. This means making it easy for all students to navigate and interact with the materials, regardless of their physical abilities. To achieve this, provide clear instructions, make sure interactive elements are keyboard-accessible, and consider the use of assistive technologies, such as screen readers or speech recognition software.

To make your content **Understandable**, focus on clarity and simplicity. This involves organizing information logically, using headings and lists to break up text, and providing clear feedback and guidance for students throughout the learning process. Additionally, consider using plain language to explain complex concepts and avoid jargon whenever possible.

Finally, aim for **Robust** content that is compatible with various devices, platforms, and assistive technologies. This involves using standard file formats to ensure your content works well on different browsers and devices.

By embracing the POUR principles in my instructional design, I have not only made my content more accessible but I'm also able to foster a more engaging and inclusive learning environment. To do the same, evaluate your current materials, identify areas for improvement, and use the strategies outlined in this section to make necessary adjustments. Incorporate the POUR principles into your future lesson planning to maximize student agency and inclusivity, and *Effectively Design Instruction* for the students in your classroom.

Proactively Plan for Predictable Barriers in Your Classroom

As educators, one of our key responsibilities is to create an inclusive and supportive learning environment that meets the diverse needs of our students. To accomplish this, it is essential to identify and address the predictable barriers that can arise in any classroom setting. These barriers may stem from a variety of factors, including social-emotional challenges, executive functioning difficulties, and diverse learning needs. By recognizing and addressing these obstacles, you can ensure that all students have equal opportunities to succeed and flourish in their educational journey.

The chart below explores the three primary categories of predictable barriers that most teachers encounter in their classroom: social-emotional barriers, executive functioning barriers, and the barriers resulting from diverse learning needs. Each category encompasses a range of potential challenges that can impact students' academic performance, social interactions, and emotional well-being. By understanding these categories and the specific barriers within them, you can proactively design your classroom to be more inclusive, accessible, and engaging for your students.

The chart not only examines the characteristics and manifestations of each category, but it also provides practical strategies for overcoming these barriers. By implementing the principles of Universal Design for Learning (UDL) and adopting a student-centered approach, you can create a flexible and responsive classroom environment that addresses the needs of all your students.

As you read through each category, be reminded of the importance of collaborating with special education professionals, parents, and caregivers to develop targeted supports and accommodations for students who face unique challenges. This collaborative approach ensures that the strategies employed are tailored to the individual needs of each student.

The following chart aims to provide you with the knowledge and tools necessary to identify and address predictable barriers in your classroom. Through a deeper understanding of these barriers, you will be better equipped to create a more inclusive classroom space:

Social-Emotional Barriers	Social-Emotional Support
Lack of self-esteem. Students with low self-esteem may feel discouraged and less confident in their abilities. This often affects their classroom performance.	Encourage a growth mindset by praising effort and progress, not just outcomes.
Anxiety. Anxiety can manifest as test anxiety, social anxiety, or general anxiety, causing students to feel overwhelmed and limiting their ability to engage in the classroom.	Implement a safe and inclusive classroom culture in which all students feel valued and respected.
Bullying. Harassment and bullying can lead to social isolation and emotional distress, negatively impacting a student's learning experience.	Provide explicit instruction in social skills and conflict resolution techniques.
Poor social skills. Difficulty navigating social interactions can lead to conflicts with peers and difficulty working in group settings.	Offer opportunities for peer mentoring and collaboration to foster social-emotional growth.

Executive Functioning	Executive Functioning Support
Time management. Students who struggle with time management may have difficulty completing tasks or assignments within the allotted time frame.	Break tasks into smaller, manageable steps and provide clear instructions.
Planning and organization. Struggles with planning and organization may lead to disorganized work, missed deadlines, and difficulty understanding and breaking down complex tasks.	Use graphic organizers and visual aids to help students with planning and organization.
Working memory. Difficulty retaining and manipulating information can hinder a student's ability to understand and follow instructions or solve problems.	Use visual aids, such as diagrams or graphic organizers, to help students organize and remember information.
Task initiation. Procrastination or difficulty starting tasks can lead to incomplete assignments and reduced engagement in learning activities.	Incorporate time management tools such as timers, schedules, and checklists.
Inhibition. Struggles with impulse control can result in disruptive behavior, difficulty following rules, and challenges with maintaining focus.	Teach self-monitoring and self-regulation strategies to help students manage their impulses and adapt to new situations.
Cognitive flexibility. Difficulty adapting to new situations, rules, or strategies can make it challenging for students to adjust to changes in the classroom environment or curriculum.	Providing students with choices can help them develop their decision-making skills and become more comfortable with making choices. This can also help them learn to adapt to different situations and make changes when needed.

Diverse learning needs	Learning Ability Support
Dyslexia. Difficulty with reading and decoding text can create barriers to understanding written material and engaging in class discussions or assignments.	Provide multisensory instruction to accommodate different learning styles and abilities.
Dyscalculia. Struggles with mathematical concepts and number sense can hinder a student's ability to grasp math-related lessons and complete assignments.	Offer assistive technology and tools, such as text-to-speech software or calculator apps, to support students with learning challenges.
Attention Deficit Hyperactivity Disorder (ADHD). Students with ADHD may have difficulty maintaining focus, staying organized, and controlling impulses, which can affect their overall classroom performance.	Allowing for movement breaks can help students with ADHD release excess energy and refocus their attention. This can include taking short breaks to stretch, walk around the room, or do other physical activities.
Autism Spectrum Disorder (ASD). Students with ASD may face challenges in social interaction, communication, and sensory processing, affecting their ability to engage and participate in classroom activities.	Collaborate with special education professionals and utilize Individualized Education Plans (IEPs) or 504 plans to provide targeted support and accommodations for students with identified needs.
Processing disorders. Slow processing speed or difficulty understanding auditory or visual information can impede a student's ability to keep up with the pace of instruction and absorb new material.	Implement differentiated instruction and flexible grouping to ensure all students are working at their appropriate skill level.

By addressing these predictable barriers and implementing a comprehensive, UDL-informed approach, you can create an inclusive learning environment that supports the diverse needs of all students. This approach will not only help your students overcome these challenges, but it will also empower them to thrive academically, socially, and emotionally.

💡 EDI Strategy: Address Learner Variability by Digitizing Resources

To effectively address learner variability and create truly inclusive classrooms, consider implementing a teaching strategy that incorporates accessible digital materials and technologies. This approach ensures that all students, regardless of their abilities or preferences, have the necessary tools to achieve independence, participation, and progress.

In today's increasingly diverse classrooms, which include a growing number of students with disabilities participating in general education, timely access to accessible digital materials and technologies is crucial for their success. Accessibility is not only the right thing to do but also a legal requirement. Providing these resources guarantees equal opportunities for students with disabilities to engage fully and independently in the curriculum, just like their peers without disabilities.

Keep in mind that learner variability is not limited to students with IEPs or 504 plans; every student enters the classroom with unique learning styles, preferences, and challenges. Therefore, it is vital to proactively plan for learner variability when designing student learning experiences.

Accessible digital materials and technologies offer various customization features that enhance learning experiences for everyone. For example, text-to-speech may be preferred by learners with strong auditory processing skills, while video captions can aid understanding for all learners. This is why many popular social media platforms emphasize using captions when posting videos—it increases engagement and enables viewers to process information more clearly.

I have found that integrating accessible digital materials into the LMS is an easy way to create an inclusive learning environment that addresses learner variability. When I work with teachers in this area, I have them start by exploring the available options within their LMS and identify which teaching tools best suit their students' needs. Then we use the available features to address learner variability.

By embracing accessible digital materials and technologies, you will contribute to a more inclusive and equitable educational environment where every student has the chance to succeed. In doing so, you will also empower your students to become expert learners, better preparing them for future educational and career opportunities.

Focusing on Students' Abilities, Not Disabilities

As educators, it's crucial to shift our mindset and concentrate on students' abilities rather than their disabilities. Embracing and cultivating each student's unique strengths can have a profound effect on their academic success, self-confidence, and overall well-being. By fostering an inclusive and encouraging classroom, students with disabilities can feel valued and driven to realize their full potential.

Consider the awe-inspiring journey of Dr. Temple Grandin, diagnosed with autism at the age of two. At the time of her diagnosis, autism was not well understood, and many believed that children with autism were incapable of leading successful lives. However, Temple's mother refused to accept this notion and sought out educational opportunities that catered to her daughter's unique needs.

Temple's journey was not easy; she faced social isolation and struggled with sensory overload in traditional school environments. But her mother's relentless advocacy and Temple's determination to overcome challenges led her to discover her exceptional talents in visual thinking and animal behavior.

Temple went on to earn a bachelor's degree in psychology, a master's degree in animal science, and a Ph.D. in animal science. She is now a renowned author, speaker, and professor of animal science at Colorado State University. Temple is also a leading advocate for people with autism and has helped change the way society views individuals with disabilities.

This remarkable story serves as a powerful reminder of the importance of focusing on students' abilities rather than their disabilities. As an educator, you have the opportunity to create a classroom environment that embraces diverse learning styles and encourages students to leverage their strengths.

I have had the privilege of collaborating with many exceptional special education teachers and administrators at Garnet Valley, including Ms. Terri Bracken, Mrs. Kim Hassel-Kloss, and Mr. Dan Arrison. Thanks to these committed leaders, I have observed varying yet effective strategies that underline the following key principles:

Identify each student's strengths and interests.
Understand your students on a personal level to understand their unique abilities and passions. This knowledge will enable you to tailor your instruction to meet their needs and capitalize on their strengths.

Differentiate instruction. Use a variety of teaching methods, materials, and assessments to accommodate diverse learning styles and abilities. This may include using visual aids, hands-on activities, and technology to support learning.

➡ **Promote collaboration and peer support.** Encourage students to work together and support one another in their learning. Pairing students with different abilities can foster understanding, empathy, and social skills.

➡ **Set high expectations.** Believe in your students' potential and encourage them to set ambitious goals. By maintaining high expectations, you can inspire students to push their boundaries and develop resilience in the face of challenges.

➡ **Provide ongoing support.** Be proactive in offering guidance and assistance to students with disabilities. Monitor their progress closely and adjust your instruction as needed to ensure they are continually supported in their learning journey.

By concentrating on abilities rather than disabilities, you unlock a world of empowerment and achievement for your students.

💡 EDI Strategy: Ensuring Multiple Means of Action and Expression

Picture a classroom where each student can articulate their understanding in the manner that resonates most with them, where no one is sidelined, and individuality is celebrated. This vision becomes reality when educators implement UDL's *Multiple Means of Action and Expression* and unlock the diverse strengths and learning preferences of each student.

Through a variety of assignments, assessments, and opportunities for interaction and feedback, students can take control of their learning process, develop a sense of agency, and increase motivation. This inclusive approach also helps to address diverse learning needs, ultimately leading to a more engaging and effective educational experience.

UDL's *Means of Action and Expression* emphasizes offering multiple ways for students to demonstrate their learning. From traditional exams to multimedia projects, roleplay, debates, and presentations, students can express themselves in the way that best suits their individual strengths. By providing choices in assignment formats and topics, students can take ownership of their learning and develop a better self-confidence. Furthermore, incorporating tools and technologies to reduce barriers and accommodate diverse learners ensures that every student has an equal opportunity to show what they have learned.

When supporting teachers on this topic, our Instructional Design Coaches work to implement the following actionable steps to help teachers ensure students have multiple opportunities to express their learning:

> Diversify your assessments and assignments by offering different formats and topics.
>
> Encourage interaction and feedback through peer review, class discussions, and student-led study groups.
>
> Utilize technology to support diverse learning needs, such as polling software, discussion boards, and assistive tools.
>
> Address assessment anxiety by providing clear guidelines, templates, and examples of graded work.
>
> Engage students in goal setting and strategic competency development to help them monitor their progress and growth.

Embracing these strategies in your instructional design opens doors to an inclusive learning environment where every student is empowered to achieve their fullest potential. It's more than a method; it's a celebration of individuality and a commitment to unlocking the unique brilliance within each learner.

The Lottery of Active Learning

Daniel Kahneman, a curious psychologist from Tel Aviv, had a question that kept him awake at night: why do people act irrationally when, theoretically, they should act logically?

Kahneman decided to conduct an experiment. He organized a lottery–but not just any lottery. This was a lottery with a twist. Half the participants were handed a lottery ticket with a pre-assigned number, while the other half received a blank ticket and a pen, with the instruction to choose their own lottery number.

In theory, since the lottery was a game of pure chance, each ticket–regardless of whether the number was pre-assigned or chosen by the participant–had an equal probability of winning. Therefore, all the tickets should have held the same value.

When the tickets were handed out, the room was filled with a sense of anticipation and excitement. The participants who got to choose their numbers took their time, mulling over their choices, as if there was some hidden strategy to unlock the game's chance.

Once everyone had their tickets, Kahneman threw another twist into the mix. He offered to buy back the tickets. This was where the story took an interesting turn. Participants who had chosen their own numbers demanded at least five times more money than the others for their ticket. A seemingly irrational behavior, considering the odds of winning were identical for each ticket.

Why did this happen?

Kahneman's experiment highlighted the inherent value people place on ownership. They treasure what they create or choose, regardless of its objective worth.

Now, imagine applying this principle to education. If students feel ownership over their learning process, if they're allowed to choose and influence their educational journey, wouldn't they become more invested and engaged? The value of active learning comes alive when students participate in shaping their education.

Consider the impact of offering students choices in their projects, topics, or methods of learning. Encourage them to "choose their numbers" in the classroom lottery, and you may find a renewed sense of excitement and commitment.

Remember, every team, classroom, or organization is a lottery of sorts. But the winning ticket might just be the one where people are allowed to make their own choices. So, are you letting your students, team, or members choose their numbers?

💡 EDI Strategy: Ensuring Multiple Means of Engagement

Fostering a sense of engagement and motivation in students is crucial for their success in the learning process. UDL recognizes the importance of engagement through the principle of "Multiple Means of Engagement." This principle emphasizes providing diverse opportunities for student involvement, catering to different motivations, learning preferences, and challenges. By offering various means of engagement, educators can account for the diverse motivations, interests, and preferences of their students.

This principle encompasses offering different levels of challenge, fostering collaboration and community, and supporting self-regulation in learning. In a classroom that embraces multiple means of engagement, students feel challenged, excited, and motivated, leading to better learning outcomes. Three ways to provide for *Multiple Means of Engagement* include providing options for:

☞ **Recruiting Student Interest**

+ Optimize individual choice and autonomy
+ Optimize relevance, value, and authenticity
+ Minimize threats and distractions

☞ **Sustaining Effort & Persistence**

+ Heighten salience of goals and objectives
+ Vary demands and resources to optimize challenge
+ Foster collaboration and community
+ Increase mastery-oriented feedback

☞ **Self-Regulation**

+ Promote expectations and beliefs that optimize motivation
+ Facilitate personal coping skills and strategies
+ Develop self-assessment and reflection

Take, for example, Mrs. Clark, a passionate high school math teacher in Allen Park School District (Wayne County, Michigan). While working with Mrs. Clark, she voiced her concern that some of her students were struggling to engage with the material, while others seemed bored and disinterested. Mrs. Clark was determined to find a solution that would make her classroom a more inclusive and engaging space for all her students.

To address the challenges mentioned above, Mrs. Clark began to leverage the EDI Strategy Card Deck she received through her partnership with *Edvative Learning*. She began to introduce various active learning activities in her lessons, such as group problem-solving sessions and hands-on activities. She also incorporated discussions and provided multiple opportunities for practice and offered prompt feedback to help her students grow.

At the same time, Mrs. Clark worked to create a more inclusive class climate, where students felt comfortable sharing their thoughts and collaborating with their peers. She introduced group projects and partnered students with different strengths to help them learn from each other. She started incorporating technology for the first time and saw that it added more interest and enhanced her students' overall learning experience. And once comfortable with her own technology skills, she created online discussion boards for students to ask questions and share insights.

To cater to different learning preferences, Mrs. Clark offered optional units in her curriculum, allowing students to explore topics that interested them most. She also encouraged student-led presentations on various math concepts which fostered more student ownership. Her journey from teaching in a typical math classroom to leading a vibrant learning environment shows the transformational power of UDL's *Multiple Means of Engagement* principle.

Mrs. Clark's story symbolizes the essence of *Effectively Designed Instruction*. By embracing the power of choice, individualization, and engagement, she created an environment in which every student could reach their full potential. Her methods and results are an inspiring testament to the power of personalized learning and the importance of allowing students to "choose their numbers."

Passions Lead to Learning

Like many teenagers, Jennie McCormick grew up with a rebellious spirit that kept her at a distance from the classroom. School didn't captivate her in the same way that sports and horseback riding did. But after relocating to Auckland, New Zealand, and stumbling upon a job as a stable hand, Jennie's fascination with the stars was ignited.

Mesmerized by the night's stars, she began attending a lecture at the Stardome Observatory and found herself awestruck by the celestial wonders of stars, planets, and galaxies. The more she learned, the deeper her thirst for knowledge became. Attending additional lectures and joining the Auckland Astronomical Society, Jennie found kindred spirits who shared her passion for the cosmos.

Jennie's passion for astronomy eventually transformed from a hobby to a profession when she was offered a part-time job at the Stardome, assisting with school group tours. This opportunity led her to establish AstroKids, a small business aimed at instilling her love for the night sky in young students. Her dedication and expertise didn't go unnoticed, and in 1998 she was offered a full-time position at the Stardome. But Jennie's journey didn't stop there.

Driven by her insatiable curiosity, Jennie and her partner embarked on a mission to build their own observatory in their backyard in east Auckland. The Farm Cove Observatory became a haven for Jennie to observe faint objects through a telescope, all while tending to her young children and hosting the Astronomy Hour talkback show on Newstalk ZB during the midnight hour.

Jennie's story serves as a testament to the transformative power of following one's passion, even in the absence of a traditional education. Her journey from casual stargazer to renowned astronomer demonstrates that education is not confined to the walls of a school. It's a reminder that curiosity, perseverance, and self-belief can overcome obstacles and lead to extraordinary discoveries.

Her life lessons emphasize the importance of initiative, seizing opportunities, and trusting intuition. Moreover, her story resonates with the core values of this chapter and the theme of accessibility and inclusion as it illustrates that there are endless avenues for learning. Jennie McCormick's journey reminds us that we all have the ability to shape our destinies and that the pursuit of passion can lead to fulfillment beyond traditional paths.

🔆 EDI Strategy: Ensuring Multiple Means of Representation

Jennie McCormick's inspiring journey into the world of astronomy underscores the transformative power of passion-driven learning. Her story emphasizes the importance of providing learners with various pathways to discovery, mirroring the Universal Design for Learning (UDL) principle of *Multiple Means of Representation*.

This principle recognizes that students come from diverse backgrounds with unique learning preferences and needs. It's about offering not only different formats of materials but also various pedagogical approaches to teaching a concept or topic. By doing so, we can ensure that all students have the opportunity to access, engage with, and make sense of what is being taught, much like how Jennie found her way into the world of celestial wonders Here are some helpful strategies to implement this principle effectively:

> **Accessible course materials:** Use common file formats, provide accessible resources, and enable closed captioning for videos.
>
> **Multimodal sources of information:** Supplement lectures and readings with visual aids, animations, and interactive elements.
>
> **Pedagogical approaches:** Employ different approaches to topics or concepts, such as case studies, testimonials, or multiple perspectives.
>
> **Student-created materials:** Encourage students to create their own graphic organizers, concept maps, or glossaries.

> 👉 **Comprehension and key concepts:** Clearly outline course outcomes and expectations, and provide practice exercises and solutions.
>
> 👉 **Check for understanding:** Summarize key points, use active learning strategies, and incorporate student response systems to gauge comprehension.

By incorporating these strategies, we can forge a learning environment that becomes more inclusive, engaging, and supportive for all students, regardless of their diverse backgrounds or needs. This endeavor requires an intentional focus on a process marked by evaluation, adaptation, and flexibility, mirroring the explorative spirit that defined Jennie's unique educational journey.

This thoughtful approach recognizes that traditional educational pathways are not the only avenues for growth and discovery. Like Jennie's profound passion for stargazing, every student's unique interest has the potential to ignite a lifelong love for learning. In fostering these passions and allowing multiple means of representation, we not only embrace diversity but also support all students in achieving their full potential, enabling them to reach for the stars, both metaphorically and literally.

> Every student's unique interest has the potential to ignite a lifelong love for learning.

Leaving the Labels Behind

When Jim Kwik was a boy living in Westchester, New York, he would pedal his bike tirelessly around the town, driven by a childlike belief that his hometown held a secret school for superheroes—the school of

151

X-Men. To him, these superheroes were more than just characters in his beloved comic books. They were misfits, outsiders, just like him.

At nine years old, Jim was labeled "the boy with the broken brain." The moniker was not a cruel taunt from his peers but a damning statement by one of Jim's teachers. This was after a severe accident had left Jim struggling to learn and making school a painfully arduous experience. After the accident, Jim's thought process was different, and it took him longer than his peers to grasp concepts. Like a lot of kids, he would often find himself pretending to understand just to fit in and please his teachers.

Jim's desperation became his inspiration and a guiding force that led him to college. This was a fresh start and a chance for him to outrun the shadow of the "broken brain" identity. But despite his determination, the challenges persisted. His college life became a tormenting period of extreme stress and strain, leading to a second head injury after a fall down a flight of stairs.

Waking up in the hospital, the sight of a mug with Albert Einstein's image and quote triggered something within him:

"The same level of thinking that created your problem won't solve your problem."

Those words resonated deeply with Jim. He realized his problem was not the "broken brain," but his perception of it. His mind might have worked differently, but that did not mean it couldn't work efficiently, even brilliantly. It sparked a profound question within him: "How do I make my brain a better brain, a super brain?"

Years later, Jim became an inspiration, not *in spite* of his so-called "broken brain," but *because* of it. His learning struggles pushed him to master the most advanced learning techniques which he now uses to train world-class entrepreneurs, Fortune 500 billionaires, past presidents, and superstars on how to improve brain performance. Jim has dedicated his life to sharing his newfound knowledge with the world.

He created his own "superhero school," where he helps others break through their learning limitations and unleash their true potential.

Jim Kwik's journey is a testament that one's struggles can become the catalyst for extraordinary accomplishments. His story reminds us that we, as educators, must remain open and flexible to the diverse learning paths our students may follow. By inspiring our students to overcome their struggles, we can help them discover their unique superpowers, embracing a philosophy that extends beyond labels and embraces the individual.

EDI Strategy: Applying Accommodations and Modification

Jim Kwik's story illustrates the importance of recognizing and honoring individual differences in the learning process. As educators, we must proactively plan and adapt our methods to ensure an inclusive and accessible learning environment for all students.

Throughout this book, I have emphasized the need to proactively plan for the predictable barriers that may limit students' ability to comprehend content. By *Effectively Designing Instruction*, you'll be able to address most students' needs. But sometimes, design alone may not be enough.

Either through a student's IEP, 504 plan, or through your own experience and expertise, there may be times when you'll need to apply further accommodations and modifications. This intricate approach to personalizing learning isn't just about adapting lessons; it's about making mindful, informed decisions that align with the unique needs of each student. Many educators, special and general educators alike, are confused by these two terms, so I want to provide a simple summation:

153

- **Accommodations** keep standards of learning the same while changing the learning approach. Examples include teacher-provided notes, allowing type-written work, preferential seating, and extended time on assignments.
- **Modifications** change the level of instruction. Examples include reduction of homework, omitting story problems, or the use of a calculator to solve problems.

Informed decision-making regarding accommodations and modifications is critical for ensuring successful and meaningful participation of students with disabilities in instruction and assessments. Ideally, these decisions will be made by the IEP team and not left to the discretion of individual teachers. However, there may be times when you will be required to go at it alone. In those instances, it's crucial to be well-equipped with the knowledge and tools that can support personalized learning for your students.

From my own experience working closely with students and navigating these waters, I identified several strategies that have proven successful when creating accommodations and modifications. Below is a chart that outlines these strategies:

Teaching Strategy	Accommodation Example	Modification Example
Lecture-Based Learning	Provide guided notes or outlines to help with note-taking.	Simplify key concepts and provide visual aids.
Group Projects	Assign roles that align with students' abilities and interests.	Form groups that cater to different learning levels.

Teaching Strategy	Accommodation Example	Modification Example
Independent Study	Allow extra time or provide reference materials.	Provide guided study with step-by-step instructions.
Hands-On Activities	Provide alternative materials for tactile learners.	Adjust activity complexity according to skill level.
Technology Integration	Utilize assistive tech, like speech-to-text.	Offer alternative software with a simpler interface.
Reading Assignments	Offer audiobooks or large print for visual impairments.	Provide reading materials at different reading levels.
Writing Assignments	Allow voice recording or typing instead of handwriting.	Simplify writing prompts or provide visual guides.
Oral Presentations	Provide visual cues or allow written reports instead of oral.	Adjust presentation complexity or length.
Assessment & Testing	Allow extended time, breaks, or quiet space for tests.	Offer different testing formats, such as multiple choice.

By implementing these strategies and finding those that work best for each individual student, you can foster an inclusive learning environment that adapts to the needs of all students. Remember, these methods are flexible, and they can be mixed and tailored according to the unique challenges and abilities of each student.

This hands-on approach not only supports students' educational journeys but also aligns with our shared goal of moving beyond traditional boundaries to create learning experiences that truly resonate with every individual.

Reflecting on Accessibility and Inclusion

In this chapter, we learned that accessibility and inclusion are key pieces in education for fostering a learning environment that caters to the unique abilities, experiences, and skill sets of all students. We explored the POUR principles (Perceivable, Operable, Understandable, and Robust) which provide a foundation for creating accessible materials that ensure all learners can perceive, navigate, and comprehend content, as well as utilize a range of current and future technologies, including assistive technologies.

We acknowledged that recognizing learner variability is essential, because it drives educators to proactively design personalized instruction for every student. The Universal Design for Learning (UDL) framework recognizes that students differ in how they perceive and comprehend information, engage with content, and express their understanding. Thus, it is vital to provide multiple means of representation, engagement, and active expression to accommodate diverse learning styles and preferences.

Finally, we recognized that adaptations, accommodations, and modifications should be individualized for students based on their needs, personal learning styles, and interests. As educators, we must be prepared to make changes in curriculum, presentation, classroom setting, and student evaluation to create an inclusive learning environment. By embracing the strategies in the accessibility and inclusion theme, teachers can support the success of all learners, regardless of their abilities or backgrounds.

As you reflect on the information presented in this chapter, consider the following questions:

1. Using the example of teachers at Adlai E. Stevenson High School, how can you create a more accessible and inclusive learning environment for all the students in your classroom?

2. After learning more about the potential challenges that can impact students' academic performance, social interactions, and emotional well-being, what steps can you take to proactively design your classroom to be more inclusive, accessible, and engaging for your students?

3. How can you embrace the principles of UDL, similar to how Mrs. Clark transformed her classroom into a vibrant, inclusive, and engaging learning environment?

4. What can you do to address the diverse needs, abilities, and experiences of your students, as Pierre du Pont did when redesigning Longwood Gardens?

5. Reflecting on Jim Kwik's journey and your own experiences, how can you inspire your students to overcome their struggles, transform their weaknesses into strengths, and help them discover their unique abilities?

6. In considering accommodations and modifications, what strategies can you implement in your classroom to ensure that learning is tailored to each student's individual needs, and how can you involve other stakeholders in this process, such as the IEP team or other educators.

CHAPTER V

~

Connecting the Dots

"Knowing is not enough; we must apply.
Willing is not enough; we must do."

–Johann Wolfgang von Goethe

This marks my 26th year working in education. Consequently, I'm fully aware that if you work in education, in any form, chances are that you have too much to do, with too little time in which to do it. So, I want to begin this final chapter by saying THANK YOU for giving up a portion of your time to read this book.

I wrote this book to help educators explore the practical strategies and innovative approaches that have empowered others to rise above the challenges of modern education. I know it's possible to create a learning environment in which both teachers and students can thrive. It's certainly not easy, but it's my hope that with the research-based strategies and approaches discussed in this book, you can *Effectively Design Instruction* and create effective and engaging learning experiences adaptable to any learning format. To do so, you'll first need to recognize and embrace the final two elements of this book: *Letting Go of Old Habits* and *It's Not Too Late to Take Your Moonshot.*

Letting Go of Old Habits

One of the first exercises I introduce when engaging with new teachers involves a simple request: "Draw a house." The details are left entirely up to them, but the task must be completed in a handful of seconds. Upon completion, a familiar pattern emerges. Most teachers sketch a square house adorned with a centrally placed door and two windows on each side. The roof is almost always triangular in shape. To be fair, when I first did this exercise, my house resembled this exact drawing. But why?

This image, despite its ubiquity, is far from the reality of our diverse living spaces. When asked why each member of the group drew almost exactly the same house, the collective response is usually, "That's how we've always drawn a house; that's how we were taught." This seemingly innocuous exercise uncovers a deep-seated issue in education:

> *The hardest part about system change isn't adopting a new mindset;*
> *it's letting go of the old one.*

Despite the struggles experienced during the pandemic, we cannot underestimate the impact virtual learning had on schools during this time. With teachers returning to school having access to new technology tools and unique expertise teaching in a virtual environment, many educational experts predict a "new normal" in how teachers deliver instruction and support students in the future.

In Garnet Valley, the pandemic reminded us that just because a student was successful in our traditional face-to-face classroom, there was no guarantee the results would be the same in the virtual environment. We also saw the opposite phenomenon as our schools began to reopen. One thing was clear: students are unique individuals, and if we were to personalize the learning experience for every one of them, we needed to continue to provide opportunities for students to have some control over their time, space, place, and pace of learning.

Following the lessons from the pandemic, our high school was able to leverage virtual learning and move to later start times that aligned with adolescent sleep study research (e.g, Hansen, et al., 2005, Fredriksen, et al., 2004, and Owens, et al., 2010).

. By creating a virtual first period, students in the Garnet Valley High School take four 70-minute face-to-face classes with 60-minutes of asynchronous classwork occurring each day. The types of asynchronous assignments vary based on the teacher, content area, and grade level of the student; however, many asynchronous activities include video presentations of new content, project-based group activities, and individualized remediation and enrichment activities. Garnet Valley High School's schedule intends to provide students with more autonomy over their learning during the school day and provide teachers with more opportunities to engage with students individually or in small groups.

As schools look to adopt similar schedules in the future and more teachers begin to offer online and blended learning opportunities to students, I believe this book will help support these shifts.

Our Next Shift: AI in Education

The latest buzz around Artificial Intelligence (AI) brings this issue into sharp focus. Pioneering AI systems like OpenAI's ChatGPT, Microsoft's Bing, and Google's Bard are revolutionizing the world at an unprecedented pace. AI has been featured in numerous media outlets, including 60 Minutes, ABC News, and TED Talks. Since ChatGPT became publicly available in November 2022, it has been adopted faster than any software tool in history, with over 100 million users to date. But as someone who has been involved in education for years, my real fear for AI in education is that this new technology will radically change the world, while education systems will be slow to adapt, or worse, not adapt at all.

AI presents various opportunities to revolutionize education. AI-powered tools can offer differentiated instruction by observing students' progress, providing help when they struggle, or delivering more challenging tasks when they master content too quickly. Intelligent textbooks like the "Inquire" iPad app developed by Stanford researchers can monitor students' focus and attention while they read, offering interactive text with key definitions, highlighting and annotation capabilities, and suggested materials tailored to students' needs and interests.

Currently, technologies like Duolingo and Reach Every Reader use AI to create and score tests and academic games that can efficiently and accurately assess students' abilities and weaknesses. These technologies will soon help promote more equitable learning by providing personalized learning experiences tailored to students' needs and learning styles.

Despite the many advantages of AI in education, there are several challenges we must still address. Dependence on these systems can cause students to become overly reliant on AI and neglect traditional learning approaches that promote critical thinking, creativity, and social skills. Privacy concerns arise regarding how AI collects, stores, and uses student data, as schools have become easy prey for cyber criminals.

If not regulated, AI systems can also perpetuate bias and discrimination if the algorithms and data sets used to train them are poorly managed. Additionally, implementing AI technology in schools will undoubtedly be expensive, because few educators have the expertise to integrate AI into their existing systems. This can create a more significant gap between schools that can afford to invest in AI technology and those that cannot, exacerbating existing inequalities in the education system.

For those of us who have been in education for a while, we remember the promise of personal computers. In the 80s and 90s, computers were seen as a way to level the playing field in education and provide all students with access to technology. However, computers and internet access are expensive, and as we saw during the pandemic, many schools and students did not have the resources needed to learn virtually.

Similarly, No Child Left Behind and standardized testing were meant to provide a way to measure student performance and hold schools and teachers more accountable. However, instead of achieving growth, we saw a narrow curriculum prioritizing test-taking skills over deeper learning and critical thinking. Even more recently, with the pandemic, schools were supposed to embrace the "next" normal, where every student had access to high-quality online and blended learning courses. But what we've seen since returning from the pandemic is a harkening back to teacher-centered classrooms.

My primary concern regarding AI in education is that while this cutting-edge technology may revolutionize the world, our education systems may not be able to keep up or, even worse, may not want to keep up. If our education systems fail to keep up with the pace of this technological change, students will fall behind, and existing inequalities will widen even further. As educators, we must advocate for the integration of AI technology into the education system in a responsible and equitable manner while at the same time ensuring that traditional learning approaches are not neglected. Only then can we ensure that AI truly transforms education and provides a better future for our students.

But AI is just the latest example. There have been and will continue to be disruptions to the way we design and deliver education to students. Like the habitual drawing of the square house, we need to critically examine our ingrained educational practices. These practices need to evolve to ensure that we provide a holistic and inclusive educational experience for students who seemingly have a world of information at their fingertips.

I am confident that with an intentional focus on instructional design, we can create an effective and engaging learning environment and *Effectively Design Instruction* for our students. But first, we'll need to take our Moonshot!

It's Never Too Late to Take Your Moonshot

I am extremely lucky to work in an organization that sets enormously high standards, embraces a growth mindset, and accepts creative tension as part of the change process. I am also well aware that this is uncommon in most school districts. I'm a firm believer that 21st-century challenges need 21st-century approaches; however, it's been my experience that school leaders are often quick to adopt minor improvements to existing systems in lieu of larger changes that would upset the status quo. But in today's fast-paced and complex educational environment, the stakes are too high, and millions of families are counting on our educational system to deliver. Minor improvements and advancements to the system are still important, but what is needed in the current state of education are more moonshots!

What is Moonshot Thinking?

Moonshot thinking is going 10x bigger or better. While many organizations try to improve by 10%, organizations that think outside the box and strive for 10x better tend to approach problems in dramatically different ways and—more times than not—achieve 10x better results. Over fifty years ago, President John F. Kennedy said, "We choose to go to the moon not because it is easy, but because it is hard." Today, this approach inspires people throughout the world to accept the enormous challenge of solving many of the world's problems; not by making small improvements to an existing system but by offering new and radical solutions to what many would consider impossible. People like

Steve Jobs (Apple), Elon Musk (Space X), Reshma Saujani (Girls Who Code), and Katherine Johnson (Hidden Figures) all exemplify what it means to think at this scale.

In the education field, we can find inspiration in the work of Salman Khan, who founded Khan Academy, a nonprofit that revolutionized online education by offering free, world-class education to anyone, anywhere. Another example is Sugata Mitra's "Hole in the Wall" experiment, which led to the concept of minimally invasive education and demonstrated the potential for self-organized learning among children.

All of these examples use a design thinking framework to find radical solutions to solve the world's biggest challenges.

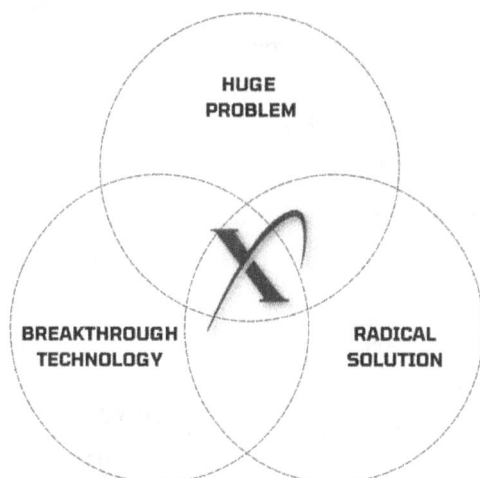

In the example of Google X Lab, it's their mission to invent and launch moonshot technologies that they hope will someday make our world a better place. Their blueprint to "solve for X" is relatively simple: identify a major problem in the world and find a radical solution that utilizes a breakthrough technology. As educators, we can take inspiration from this approach and apply it to our classrooms to revolutionize education for the students we serve.

Why Moonshot Thinking is Needed in Education Now More than Ever

Many classroom teachers and school leaders are hampered by poor educational policies, cash-hungry textbook publishers, and a school system that is often slow to adopt innovation. Waiting for the federal or state legislature to "fix" education often results in endless finger-pointing and little in the way of results. So, if we are truly going to prepare students for *their futures*, it is time we all start thinking 10x bigger.

The road ahead will certainly be paved with difficulties and challenges, but as Burt Rutan said after winning the $10 million XPRIZE in 2005, "The day before something is truly a breakthrough, it's a crazy idea." I'm sure creating a lower-cost, reliable, reusable, privately financed, crewed spaceship that made private space travel commercially viable, sounded like a crazy idea in 2005. OK, to be honest, it still does, but because Burt Rutan and his team thought 10x bigger, the likes of three space barons—Jeff Bezos, Richard Branson, and Elon Musk—are now at the forefront of the space travel industry. With vision and leadership, the once crazy idea of personalized learning for all students is absolutely attainable.

Our students deserve an educational experience that is ten times better, not just ten percent improved. Moonshot thinking is needed because it has the potential to revolutionize the way we approach education, making it more inclusive, adaptive, and engaging for all students, regardless of their background or learning style.

> Our students deserve an educational experience that is ten times better, not just ten percent improved.

At Garnet Valley, we used moonshot thinking to break free from the constraints of traditional educational models and create learning environments that truly empower students and foster their creativity, curiosity, and passion for learning. Through *intentional* instructional design, you can pave the way for a brighter and more equitable education experience for all students. So, let's take that leap, embrace the challenge, and aim for the moon—our students deserve nothing less!

Notes & References

Preface

- Rose, T. (2016). *The End of Average: How We Succeed in a World That Values Sameness.* Harper One.
- No Child Left Behind (NCLB) Act of 2001, Pub. L. No. 107-110, § 101, Stat. 1425 (2002).
- Danielson Group. (n.d.). Framework. Danielson Group. Retrieved from https://danielsongroup.org/framework/
- Murray, T. C. (2019). *Personal & Authentic: Designing Learning Experiences That Impact a Lifetime.*

Introduction

- UNESCO. (2020). *COVID-19 education response.* https://en.unesco.org/covid19/educationresponse/globalcoalition
- Hamilton, L. S., Grant, D., Kaufman, J. H., Diliberti, M., Schwartz, H. L., Hunter, G. P., Messan Setodji, C., & Young, C. J. (2020). *COVID-19 and the state of K–12 schools: Results and technical documentation from the spring 2020 American educator panels COVID-19 surveys.* RAND Research Report. https://www.rand.org/pubs/research_reports/RRA168-1.html

- Novak, K., & Chardin, M. (2021). *Equity by Design: delivering on the power and promise of UDL*. Thousand Oaks, California, Corwin Press, Inc.
- CAST. (n.d.). Universal Design for Learning (UDL) guidelines. Retrieved from http://www.cast.org/our-work/about-udl.html
- McTighe, J., & Wiggins, G. (n.d.). Understanding by Design (UbD). ASCD. Retrieved from http://www.ascd.org/research-a-topic/understanding-by-design.aspx
- ASCD. Retrieved from http://www.ascd.org/research-a-topic/differentiated-instruction-resources.aspx
- Zemeckis, R. (Director). (1985). *Back to the Future* [Film]. Universal Pictures.

Theme: Designing Experiences

- Apollo 13. (1970). NASA. Retrieved from https://www.nasa.gov/
- The Disney Institute, Kinni, T., & Disney Imagineers. (2011). Be Our Guest: Perfecting the Art of Customer Service. Disney Editions.
- Calvo-Lopez, J., Luna-Aranda, R., & Rabasco, A. (2014). The Great Mosque of Cordoba: Geometric Analysis and Architectural Reconstruction. Nexus Network Journal, 16(3), 639-654.
- Reading Rockets. (n.d.). Rudine Sims Bishop on Mirrors, Windows, and Sliding Doors. YouTube. Retrieved from https://www.youtube.com/watch?v=_AAu58SNSyc
- Kahneman, D., & Fredrickson, B. L. (1993). When more pain is preferred to less: Adding a better end. Psychological Science, 4(6), 401-405.
- United Nations. (n.d.). Sustainable Development Goals. Retrieved from https://sdgs.un.org/goals

- Spencer, J., & Juliani, A.J. (2017). Empower: What Happens When Students Own Their Learning. IMpress Books.
- Louis Deslauriers. Deslauriers, L., Schelew, E., & Wieman, C. (2019). Improved learning in a large-enrollment physics class. Proceedings of the National Academy of Sciences, 116(39), 19251-19257. doi: 10.1073/pnas.1821936116
- Juliani, A.J. (n.d.). *The Ultimate Guide to Choice Boards and Learning Menus* [Blog post]. Retrieved from [URL]
- Reid, J. (2018, May 22). How to Scale a Magical Experience: 4 Lessons from Airbnb's Brian Chesky [Blog post]. Retrieved from https://reid.medium.com/how-to-scale-a-magical-experience-4-lessons-from-airbnbs-brian-chesky-eca0a182f3e3

Theme: Building Interactions

- Columbia University's Center for Teaching and Learning (CTL) is a prominent institute committed to advancing innovative and effective teaching practices and technologies to enhance learning. The CTL partners with faculty, students, and colleagues across the University to support excellence and innovation in teaching and learning.
- Hattie, J., & Clinton, J. (2008). Identifying accomplished teachers: A validation study. In *Assessing teachers for professional certification: The first decade of the National Board for Professional Teaching Standards* (Vol. 11, pp. 313-344). Emerald Group Publishing Limited.
- Youth Truth is a national non-profit organization that harnesses student and stakeholder feedback to help educators and school leaders accelerate improvements in their K-12 schools and classrooms.

+ Johnson, D.W., Johnson, R.T., & Holubec, E. J. (1998). *Cooperation in the classroom* (pp. 4-7). Boston, MA, USA: Allyn and Bacon Publishing.

+ Saucier, D. A., Miller, S. S., Jones, T. L., & Martens, A. L. (2022). Trickle down Engagement: Effects of Perceived Teacher and Student Engagement on Learning Outcomes. *International Journal of Teaching and Learning in Higher Education, 33*(2), 168-179. Cooper, K. S. (2014). Eliciting engagement in the high school classroom: A mixed-methods examination of teaching practices. *American educational research journal, 51*(2), 363-402.

+ Volkswagen. (2009). *The Fun Theory.* http://www.thefuntheory.com/

Theme: Presenting Content

+ The phrase "form follows function" is often attributed to the American architect Louis Sullivan. He first used this phrase in an article titled "The Tall Office Building Artistically Considered," published in Lippincott's Magazine in March 1896.

+ Quality Matters. (n.d.). QM K-12 rubric. Quality Matters. https://www.qualitymatters.org/qa-resources/rubric-standards

+ Mormando, S. E. (2022). *Special Education Itinerant Teacher Engagement with Students Enrolled in Blended Learning Classes Post Pandemic.* Widener University.

+ *The Jetsons* was an American animated sitcom that was originally aired from 1962 to 1963 and was later revived in the mid-1980s. It was one of the first programs ever broadcast in color on ABC.

+ Gonzalez, J. (2018, October 21). Are You a Curator or a Dumper? Cult of Pedagogy. https://www.cultofpedagogy.com/curator-or-dumper/

Theme: Accessibility and Inclusion

- CAST (2018). Universal Design for Learning Guidelines version 2.2. Retrieved from http://udlguidelines.cast.org
- Kwik, J. (2020). *Limitless: Upgrade Your Brain, Learn Anything Faster, and Unlock*
- *Your Exceptional Life.* Hay House.
- Johnson, C. (2022, February 4). How Jennie McCormick went from casual stargazing to discovering extrasolar planets. *NZ Life & Leisure Magazine.*
- Kahneman, D. (2011). *Thinking, Fast and Slow.* Macmillan.
- Smith, J. (2022, August 10). Designing Accessibility: POUR. AEM Center. https://aem.cast.org/create/designing-accessibility-pour
- Accessibility Guidelines Working Group (AG WG) Participants. (2018). Understanding the Four Principles of Accessibility. Web Accessibility Initiative (WAI). Copyright © 2010 W3C® (MIT, ERCIM, Keio). Co-Chairs: Alastair Campbell, Charles Adams, Rachael Bradley Montgomery. https://www.w3.org/TR/WCAG21/

Connecting the Dots

- Fredriksen, K., Rhodes, J., Reddy, R., & Way, N. (2004). Sleepless in Chicago: tracking the effects of adolescent sleep loss during the middle school years. Child development, 75(1), 84-95.
- Hansen, M., Janssen, I., Schiff, A., Zee, P. C., & Dubocovich, M. L. (2005). The impact of school daily schedule on adolescent sleep. *Pediatrics,* 115(6), 1555-1561.
- Owens, J. A., Belon, K., & Moss, P. (2010). Impact of delaying school start time on adolescent sleep, mood, and behavior. *Archives of pediatrics & adolescent medicine,* 164(7), 608-614.

- Mormando,S.E.(2018,January8).Therearenotenoughmoonshots taken in education. *eSchoolNews*. https://www.eschoolnews.com/ educational-leadership/2018/01/08/not-enough-moonshots-taken-education/
- Google X Lab, also known as X, is a secretive facility owned by Alphabet Inc., Google's parent company. It focuses on developing futuristic technology and moonshot projects. X has worked on various ambitious projects, such as self-driving cars, Project Loon for providing internet access through high-altitude balloons, and Google Glass. X aims to create revolutionary advancements that may not be commercially viable yet, but have the potential to solve significant global problems. Through continuous experimentation and innovation, X is driving the development of groundbreaking technologies for a better future.

Acknowledgments

Garnet Valley School District

My colleagues at Garnet Valley, from my "Hallway Team," to my colleagues in the classroom, have provided me with daily inspiration and brought out the best in me. I am both grateful and honored to have the privilege to work alongside such an extraordinary team.

At the heart of this incredible team stands our Superintendent of Schools, Dr. Marc Bertrando, a beacon of leadership and a true master of his craft. His vision, wisdom, and relentless pursuits of excellence have not only shaped our district but have also inspired all who have had the honor to work under his guidance. His ability to see potential, foster growth, and lead with integrity is unparalleled, and it makes him not just the best at what he does, but one of the most authentic mentors and role models in education today.

To our amazing CI&T Team, Leslee, Kyle, Kris, and Julie, I extend my deepest gratitude. Your support, collaboration, and friendship have been instrumental in shaping not only this book but also the lives of countless students we serve. Your collective passion for education fuels my own, and I am eternally thankful for the opportunity to learn from and grow with each one of you. May our shared mission continue to thrive, and may our collective efforts keep igniting the spark of learning in the hearts and minds of those we are privileged to teach.

I must also extend my profound appreciation to our school board members, whose tireless efforts and steadfast commitment ensure that every student matters. Their decisions, always made with the best interest of the school community in mind, reflect a deep understanding of our shared mission and a genuine care for the well-being of our students. Their leadership is a testament to what can be achieved when hearts and minds are aligned in service to others.

Instructional Design Coaches

Your dedication deserves a special note of gratitude. Your roles as mentors, resident experts, and collaborators have been instrumental in shaping the educational landscape within our school community and beyond. With a keen eye for detail and a compassionate understanding of both teacher and student needs, you have worked tirelessly to elevate instructional practices.

Your commitment to professional development, your willingness to share expertise, and your relentless pursuit of excellence have not only enriched the lives of our colleagues, but have also created a ripple effect, reaching every student in our care. The impact of your work resonates far beyond the walls of our classrooms, and has fostered a culture of continuous growth and innovation with everyone you have come in contact with.

I am honored to work alongside such a talented and dedicated group of professionals. Your contributions to this book and to our shared mission are invaluable. Thank you for your unwavering support, your insightful guidance, and your steadfast belief in the power of EDI. May we continue to learn from one another and strive together to create learning environments that truly meet the needs of every student.

To My Family

To Tracy, your unwavering support and encouragement have been my guiding light. Your strength, wisdom, and love have not only nurtured our family but have also fueled my professional pursuits. I am eternally grateful for your presence in my life, and I cherish every moment we share.

To Vincent and Nicholas, your curiosity, resilience, and joy inspire me every day. Watching you grow and explore the world fills me with pride and hope. Your achievements are a testament to your character and potential. I am honored to be your father and look forward to all the adventures that await us.

To my parents, who face every challenge with grace and make the difficult seem easy, your sacrifices and dedication have shaped the person I am today. Your lessons in humility, hard work, and compassion resonate in everything I do. Your love has been my foundation, and your example continues to guide me. Thank you for the endless support, the wisdom, and the values you instilled in me.

Family is the compass that guides us, and I am profoundly blessed to have you all by my side. Your love and belief in me have made this book and all my endeavors possible. Thank you for being my constant source of inspiration, strength, and joy.

About the Author

D r. Samuel Mormando is the Director of Technology, Innovation, and Online Learning for the Garnet Valley School District in Glen Mills, Pennsylvania. Sam earned his doctorate in educational leadership from Widener University and was honored by the United States Distance Learning Association (USDLA) as the 2020 K–12 Innovation Award Winner. Under his leadership, Garnet Valley has become nationally recognized for innovative teaching practices, including its adoption of open education resources and development of a student-centered course design process that allows students to take courses in the traditional face-to-face, online, or blended formats.

In 2018, Dr. Mormando founded *Edvative Learning*, a dynamic non-profit organization with a clear vision and mission to address the evolving challenges in education. The organization initially collaborated with local school districts, focusing on online and blended learning. However, when the COVID-19 pandemic struck, *Edvative Learning* swiftly expanded its support to schools nationwide, assisting them in navigating the sudden shift to remote learning.

The formation of *Edvative Learning* stemmed from a deep understanding of the daily challenges faced by teachers. As teachers, instructional coaches, and school administrators, our team witnessed firsthand the need for practical, research-based strategies and approaches that would empower educators to create effective and engaging learning experiences. This recognition led to the development of *Edvative Learning*, and with it, a commitment to supporting educators and school leaders across the country.

The organization boasts a diverse team, comprising experienced educators, administrators, and district personnel, including Superintendents, Assistant Superintendents, Curriculum Supervisors, and Directors. This collective expertise allows *Edvative Learning* to offer comprehensive support and insights to educators at all levels.

Connect with Sam at:
email: mormans@garnetvalley.org, smormando@edvative.com
website: www.edvative.com
twitter: @SamMormando

More from ConnectEDD Publishing

Since 2015, ConnectEDD has worked to transform education by empowering educators to become better-equipped to teach, learn, and lead. What started as a small company designed to provide professional learning events for educators has grown to include a variety of services to help educators and administrators address essential challenges. ConnectEDD offers instructional and leadership coaching, professional development workshops focusing on a variety of educational topics, a roster of nationally recognized educator associates who possess hands-on knowledge and experience, educational conferences custom-designed to meet the specific needs of schools, districts, and state/national organizations, and ongoing, personalized support, both virtually and onsite. In 2020, ConnectEDD expanded to include publishing services designed to provide busy educators with books and resources consisting of practical information on a wide variety of teaching, learning, and leadership topics. Please visit us online at connecteddpublishing.com or contact us at: info@connecteddpublishing.com

Recent Publications:

Live Your Excellence: Action Guide by Jimmy Casas

Culturize: Action Guide by Jimmy Casas

Daily Inspiration for Educators: Positive Thoughts for Every Day of the Year by Jimmy Casas

Eyes on Culture: Multiply Excellence in Your School by Emily Paschall

Pause. Breathe. Flourish. Living Your Best Life as an Educator by William D. Parker

L.E.A.R.N.E.R. Finding the True, Good, and Beautiful in Education by Marita Diffenbaugh

Educator Reflection Tips Volume II: Refining Our Practice by Jami Fowler-White

Handle With Care: Managing Difficult Situations in Schools with Dignity and Respect by Jimmy Casas and Joy Kelly

Disruptive Thinking: Preparing Learners for Their Future by Eric Sheninger

Permission to be Great: Increasing Engagement in Your School by Dan Butler

Daily Inspiration for Educators: Positive Thoughts for Every Day of the Year, Volume II by Jimmy Casas

The 6 Literacy Levers: Creating a Community of Readers by Brad Gustafson

The Educator's ATLAS: Your Roadmap to Engagement by Weston Kieschnick

In This Season: Words for the Heart by Todd Nesloney, LaNesha Tabb, Tanner Olson, and Alice Lee

Leading with a Humble Heart: A 40-Day Devotional for Leaders by Zac Bauermaster

Recalibrate the Culture: Our Why…Our Work…Our Values by Jimmy Casas

Creating Curious Classrooms: The Beauty of Questions by Emma Chiappetta

Crafting the Culture: 45 Reflections on What Matters Most by Joe Sanfelippo and Jeffrey Zoul

Improving School Mental Health: The Thriving School Community Solution by Charle Peck and Dr. Cameron Caswell

Building Authenticity: A Blueprint for the Leader Inside You by Todd Nesloney and Tyler Cook

Connecting Through Conversation: A Playbook for Talking with Kids by Erika Bare and Tiffany Burns

The Dream Factory: Designing a Purposeful Life by Mark Trumbo

Stories Behind Stances: Creating Empathy Through Hearing "The Other Side" by Chris Singleton

Happy Eyes: Becoming All Things to All People by Ryan Tillman

The Generative Age: Artificial Intelligence and the Future of Education by Alana Winnick

Recalibrate the Culture: Action Guide by Jimmy Casas

Leading with PEOPLE: A Six Pillar Framework for Fruitful Leadership by Zac Bauermaster

ConnectEDD
PUBLISHING